Laurie Boswell

Richard C. Evans

Art Johnson

Gloria Robinson

Samuel Robinson

GReaT SoURCe®
EDUCATION GROUP
A Houghton Mifflin Company
New Ways to Know®

Credits

Editorial: Carol DeBold, Kathy Kellman, Susan Rogalski

Design/Production: Taurins Design, NYC

Creative Art: Debbie Tilley

Technical Art: Taurins Design, NYC

Cover and Package Design: Great Source/Kristen Davis

Today's Challenge Multiply without using a calculator. Write the answers, then put the answers in order.

1. What is $2 \times 2 \times 2$? _____

2. What is 2^3? _____

3. What is 3×2^3? _____

4. What is 5×5? _____

5. What is 5^2? _____

6. What is 3×5^2? _____

7. What is 2×7? _____

8. What is 3×7? _____

9. What is $5^2 \times 2 \times 7$? _____

10. What is $5^2 \times 2^2 \times 7$? _____

11. Write the answers to exercises 1–10 in order, from least to greatest.

_____

Go Further Find factors for the numbers. If your factors are not prime numbers, find the prime factors. Write your final answer using exponents.

Example

80	$=$	☐10 $\times$ ◯8
☐10	$=$	☐2×5
◯8	$=$	$2 \times 4 =$ ◯$2 \times 2 \times 2$
So, 80	$=$	☐2×5 $\times$ ◯$2 \times 2 \times 2$
	$=$	$2^4 \times 5$

12. Factor 24. _____

13. Factor 60. _____

14. Factor 90. _____

On today's activity: (Circle one)   I need to know more.   I got it.

Name _____   **Date** _____

Today's Challenge — Three-Digit Sum Challenge

Use the 1–9 digit cards to form two-digit addends. You are looking for three-digit sums. Each card will be used only once. Record your solutions here. *Note*: two solutions are **not** different if the two addends are switched: 268 + 497 is equivalent to 497 + 268.

On today's activity: (Circle one) — I need to know more. — I got it.

2 Name

Date

Go Further — **Three-Digit Sum Challenge**

You have found several solutions to the Three-Digit Sum Challenge. Work with a partner. Look at the solutions you have to the problem and try to discover anything that is true about all of the solutions.

Things we discovered: _____

_____

_____

_____

_____

Quite often you can find new solutions by looking at other solutions. For example, $586 + 143 = 729$ is one solution. You can find a new solution by switching the numbers in the ones place in each addend. Thus, $583 + 146 = 729$ is another solution.

$$
\begin{array}{r}
5\ 8\ \boxed{6} \\
+1\ 4\ ③ \\
\hline
7\ 2\ 9
\end{array}
\qquad
\begin{array}{r}
5\ 8\ ③ \\
+1\ 4\ \boxed{6} \\
\hline
7\ 2\ 9
\end{array}
$$

1. Take a solution you found before and find other solutions by switching two digits. How many different solutions can be found in this way? Show these new solutions. **Hint:** Think about switching 8 with 4 in the original problem shown.

    _____

    _____

    _____

2. What other things could you do to generate new solutions from one you already have?

    _____

    _____

    _____

On today's activity: (Circle one) — I need to know more. — I got it.

Name _____ **Date** _____

3

Game Time

Get Started   All quadrilaterals on this page are rectangles.

Example 1

| Perimeter: 24 meters | [rectangle] 5 m
_7_ m |

Example 2

| Perimeter: 24 meters | [rectangle] _4_ m
8 m |

Today's Challenge   Fill in the table.

1.	Perimeter: 24 feet	[rectangle] ___ ft 9 ft	**2.**	Perimeter: 24 feet	[rectangle] 1 ft ___ ft
3.	Perimeter: 24 centimeters	[square] 6 cm ___ cm	**4.**	Perimeter: 24 centimeters	[rectangle] 2 cm ___ cm
5.	Perimeter: 20 yards	[rectangle] 2 yd ___ yd	**6.**	Perimeter: 20 yards	[rectangle] 3 yd ___ yd
7.	Perimeter: 20 inches	[rectangle] ___ in. 9 in.	**8.**	Perimeter: 20 inches	[rectangle] ___ in. 6 in.
9.	Perimeter: 30 yards	[rectangle] 5 yd ___ yd	**10.**	Perimeter: 30 yards	[rectangle] 3 yd ___ yd
11.	Perimeter: 30 feet	[rectangle] 6 ft ___ ft	**12.**	Perimeter: 30 feet	[square] 7 ft ___ ft
13.	Perimeter: 36 inches	[rectangle] 8 in. ___ in.	**14.**	Perimeter: 36 inches	[rectangle] 7 in. ___ in.
15.	Perimeter: 36 centimeters	[rectangle] ___ cm 12 cm	**16.**	Perimeter: 36 centimeters	[rectangle] 5 cm ___ cm

On today's activity: (Circle one)   I need to know more.   I got it.

Name

Date

Get Started
Tony and Katia were checking their answers to a homework problem dealing with multiplication. Study the problem. Without multiplying, figure out who is correct. Explain how you knew.

Tony	Katia
182	182
× 34	× 34
4186	6188

Explanation: _____

_____

Today's Challenge — **Mark the letter of the correct answer.** Without multiplying, find the answer that makes sense for each exercise. Explain why each answer choice is correct or incorrect.

1. 428 × 35
   A. 14,982 _____
   B. 17,250 _____
   C. 12,980 _____
   D. 14,980 _____

2. 89 × 74
   A. 6586 _____
   B. 6568 _____
   C. 8526 _____
   D. 7436 _____

3. 274 × 67
   A. 15,358 _____
   B. 17,250 _____
   C. 12,858 _____
   D. 18,358 _____

4. What advice would you give to a student who is working on a multiplication test in multiple-choice format? As part of your answer, explain why it may not always be necessary to complete the multiplication.

_____

_____

On today's activity: (Circle one) — I need to know more. — I got it.

Name _____ Date _____ 5

Today's Challenge Organize these terms by putting each one in the category that best fits its definition.

1. These are terms that are related to addition or subtraction.

   _____   _____

   _____   _____

2. These are terms that are related to multiplication or division.

   _____   _____

   _____   _____

3. These are terms that are related to decimals.

   _____   _____

   _____   _____

4. These are terms that are related to fractions.

   _____   _____

   _____   _____

sum
equivalent fraction
subtrahend
divisor
place value
product
decimal point
quotient
numerator
factor
addend
denominator
base 10
difference
mixed number

Go Further

5. List five other mathematical terms that you know. Give an example for each term.

   _____   _____

   _____   _____

   _____

On today's activity: (Circle one)   I need to know more.   I got it.

Today's Challenge ✎ Multiplying by Nine

Multiplication by nine has some very interesting patterns associated with it. You will explore some of those patterns for different types of numbers.

1. **a.** 9×1 _____ **b.** 9×2 _____ **c.** 9×3 _____ **d.** 9×4 _____

   e. 9×5 _____ **f.** 9×6 _____ **g.** 9×7 _____ **h.** 9×8 _____

   i. 9×9 _____

2. **a.** 9×26 _____ **b.** 9×17 _____ **c.** 9×49 _____ **d.** 9×36 _____

3. **a.** 9×83 _____ **b.** 9×54 _____ **c.** 9×65 _____ **d.** 9×31 _____

4. **a.** 9×30 _____ **b.** 9×70 _____ **c.** 9×40 _____ **d.** 9×60 _____

5. You can multiply by nine on your hands. Number your fingers from one to ten as shown. To multiply nine by seven, bend the finger representing seven. On the left you have six fingers which represent the number of tens in the product and on the right you have three fingers which represent the number of ones in the product.

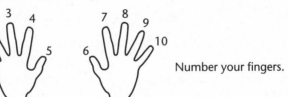

Number your fingers.

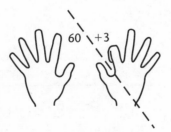

Show 7×9.

How might you use your fingers to multiply nine by a multiple of ten?

_____

_____

On today's activity: (Circle one) ✎ I need to know more. ✎ I got it.

Name _____ **Date** _____

Go Further — Multiplying by Nine

You have found the products of nine and all of the one-digit and some two-digit numbers. Work with a partner to discover things about products when one factor is nine by studying your answers to page 7.

1. Analyze the products in exercise 1. _____

_____

_____

2. Analyze the products in exercise 2. _____

_____

_____

3. Analyze the products in exercise 3. _____

_____

_____

4. Analyze the products in exercise 4. _____

_____

_____

Compare and contrast your answers to exercises 1–4 above.

Things we discovered:

_____

_____

_____

_____

_____

_____

On today's activity: (Circle one) — I need to know more. — I got it.

Today's Challenge ✐ Find strings of digits that can be used to make equivalent fractions. Record the pairs of equivalent fractions you find.

3	6	3	2
4	1	2	4
3	5	6	8
9	1	5	7

Pairs of Equivalent Fractions

_____ = _____

_____ = _____

_____ = _____

_____ = _____

Go Further ✐ Fill in the numerators to make equivalent fractions.

1. $\frac{1}{8} = \frac{\square}{16}$

2. $\frac{2}{3} = \frac{\square}{9}$

3. $\frac{5}{6} = \frac{\square}{18}$

4. $\frac{3}{4} = \frac{\square}{24}$

5. $\frac{3}{5} = \frac{\square}{100}$

6. $\frac{7}{25} = \frac{\square}{75}$

7. How did you solve exercises 1–6? Give an example and explain your thinking.

_____

_____

_____

_____

_____

On today's activity: (Circle one) ✐ I need to know more. ✐ I got it.

Name _____ Date _____ **9**

Get Started   Fill in the letters of the correct answers.

Oscar was doing his homework on adding fractions. Here are six examples of his work. Which sums are correct?

(A) _____ $\frac{2}{5} + \frac{1}{3} = \frac{3}{8}$

(B) _____ $\frac{2}{7} + \frac{3}{7} = \frac{5}{7}$

(C) _____ $\frac{3}{10} + \frac{1}{10} = \frac{4}{10}$ or $\frac{2}{5}$

(D) _____ $\frac{1}{6} + \frac{2}{3} = \frac{3}{9}$ or $\frac{1}{3}$

(E) _____ $\frac{4}{9} + \frac{1}{9} = \frac{5}{9}$

(F) _____ $\frac{3}{8} + \frac{3}{4} = \frac{6}{12}$ or $\frac{1}{2}$

Today's Challenge   For each item, write the answer you think Oscar would give, then fill in the grid with the *correct* answer in simplest form.

Exercise	Oscar's Answer	Correct Answer	Exercise	Oscar's Answer	Correct Answer	Exercise	Oscar's Answer	Correct Answer
1. $\frac{1}{5} + \frac{1}{3}$	___		2. $\frac{3}{8} + \frac{1}{8}$	___		3. $\frac{4}{9} + \frac{2}{9}$	___	
4. $\frac{2}{7} + \frac{3}{7}$	___		5. $\frac{3}{8} + \frac{1}{2}$	___		6. $\frac{1}{2} + \frac{1}{2}$	___	

7. What advice would you give Oscar about adding fractions?

_____

_____

On today's activity: (Circle one)   I need to know more.   I got it.

Name

Date

Today's Challenge Use the words from the box to match the descriptions. You will not use all of the words.

quart
pound
liter
hour
mile
teaspoon
centimeter
gallon
cup
month
yard
kilogram

1. A unit of weight in the customary system. _____

2. A unit of length in the customary system that is equal to 5280 feet. _____

3. There are three of these in one tablespoon.

   _____

4. This unit of length is equal to 36 inches.

   _____

5. This measure is eight fluid ounces. There are four in a quart. _____

6. A unit of mass in the metric system. _____

7. There are 12 of these in a year. They have 28–31 days.

   _____

8. There are 100 of these in one meter. _____

9. A unit of fluid capacity in the metric system. _____

10. Four quarts make one of these. _____

Go Further Write what you think.

11. If you saw the number 12 you might think it was eggs in a dozen, numbers on a clock, inches in a foot, or months in a year. Tell what the numbers four and ten make you think of.

   _____

   _____

On today's activity: (Circle one) I need to know more. I got it.

Name _____ **Date** _____ 11

Today's Challenge — Rectangles in a Row

Your task is to count all of the rectangles in an arrangement of 10 side-by-side squares. Remember that every square is also a rectangle. Look at the diagram.

A	B	C	D	E	F	G	H	I	J

In the figure there are many rectangles. There are some two-by-one rectangles like the ones formed by squares A and B and by squares F and G. There are even some four-by-one rectangles like the ones formed by squares B–E and by squares D–G.

To help keep track as you count the rectangles, you may want to make an organized list. Such a list has been started for you.

1. One-by-one rectangles __A, B,_____

2. Two-by-one rectangles __A–B, B–C,_____

3. _____

_____

_____

_____

_____

_____

_____

_____

4. How many rectangles are there in a row of 10 squares arranged side-by-side as shown in the diagram?

_____

On today's activity: (Circle one) — I need to know more. — I got it.

12 **Name**

Date

Go Further Rectangles in a Row

You have found the number of rectangles in a ten-by-one rectangular arrangement of squares. Work with a partner to compare your results, then list what you discovered about rectangles in a row of squares.

Things we discovered: _____

_____

_____

_____

_____

_____

_____

_____

1. If you had 21 squares in the row, what would you do to figure out how many rectangles there were?

   _____

   _____

   _____

   _____

2. Write a formula that you could use to find the number of rectangles in a row of 100 squares. What about a row of *n* squares?

   _____

   _____

   _____

On today's activity: (Circle one) I need to know more. I got it.

Name **Date**

13

Go Further Follow the directions to mark numbers in the grid. Some will be marked more than once.

30	20	8	15
24	18	32	6
70	72	66	12
54	36	50	60

1. Cross out all numbers that are multiples of ten.

2. Circle all numbers less than or equal to 6×2.

3. Star all numbers greater than the number of cents in ten nickels.

4. Underline all numbers less than or equal to the least common multiple of three and eight.

5. Box all numbers less than the number of inches in three feet and greater than the number of cups in a gallon.

6. Which number is not marked? _____

7. Write at least three statements to describe that number.

_____

_____

_____

On today's activity: (Circle one) I need to know more. I got it.

14 Name _____

Date

Get Started Drawing a diagram or using one that's been provided for you can be very helpful when solving a test problem. Solve this problem.

Line segment *AB* contains points *C, D,* and *E.* The length of $\overline{AC}$ is three centimeters, the length of $\overline{CE}$ is three centimeters, the length of $\overline{DB}$ is three centimeters, and the length of $\overline{AD}$ is four centimeters. Find the lengths of $\overline{BE}, \overline{DE},$ and $\overline{AB}.$

_____

Today's Challenge Write your answer in the space provided.

Study the diagram. There are three ways to travel from Plymouth to Concord without going through Lowell or Westford (routes *a, b,* and *c*). There are four ways to travel from Concord to Lowell without going through Plymouth or Westford (routes *w, x, y,* and *z*).

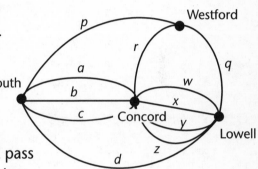

1. List all of the routes from Plymouth to Lowell that pass through Concord but not Westford. For example, try route *b* + route *x*. How many different routes are there?

_____

2. Draw a diagram that reflects these facts.
   • You can get from *A* to *D* by going through *B* or *C* but not both *B* and *C*.
   • You can get from *A* to *F* by going through both *B* and *E* or through both *B* and *D*.
   Name one other route from *A* to *F.* _____

3. What advice would you give to a student who needs help making sense of a problem?

_____

_____

_____

On today's activity: (Circle one) I need to know more. I got it.

Name _____ **Date** _____

Today's Challenge   Find my number.

1. Subtracting six from my number leaves eight. What's my number? _____

2. Seven times my number equals 56. What's my number? _____

3. Twice my number is 36. What's my number? _____

4. Half of 38 is my number. What's my number? _____

5. Three times my number is 51. What's my number? _____

6. I can multiply anything by my number and the answer will always be the same. What's my number? _____

7. Five times my number is sixty. What's my number? _____

8. $\frac{1}{5}$ of 75 is my number. What's my number? _____

9. My number is $\frac{1}{4}$ of 52. What's my number? _____

10. When you multiply my number by itself, the product is **81**. What's my number? _____

Go Further

11. Write four *What's My Number?* problems for a friend. Make your mystery numbers less than 50.

_____

_____

_____

_____

_____

_____

Friend's name _____

On today's activity: (Circle one)   I need to know more.   I got it.

  Name _____   **Date** _____

Today's Challenge   Sierpinski's Triangle

The large equilateral triangle below is considered Stage Zero.

- Find the midpoints of the sides.

- Connect the midpoints to make a new set of four equilateral triangles.

- Shade in the middle triangle.

This new set of four triangles is Stage One. Apply the directions above to the new <u>unshaded</u> triangles to complete three more stages. Record in the table the number of shaded and unshaded triangles in Stages 1–4.

Stage	0	1	2	3	4	5	6
Unshaded Triangles	1						
Shaded Triangles	0						

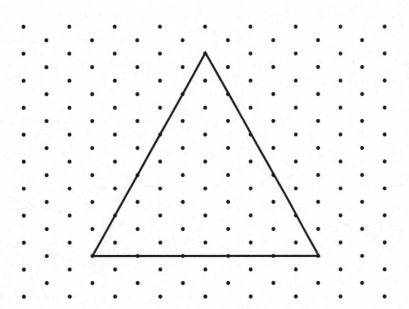

On today's activity: (Circle one)   I need to know more.   I got it.

Name   **Date**

Go Further ✎ Sierpinski's Triangle

You have found how many shaded and unshaded triangles there are for Stages One through Four. Work with a partner. Without actually drawing the triangles, figure out how many shaded and unshaded triangles there would be in Stages Five and Six. Look for patterns in the numbers you generated in Stages One through Four.

Describe the patterns you found for the shaded triangles and unshaded triangles.

Things we discovered: _____

_____

_____

_____

1. Use your pattern to figure out how many unshaded triangles are in Stage Five of Sierpinski's Triangle. _____

2. Use your pattern to figure out how many unshaded triangles are in Stage Six of Sierpinski's Triangle. _____

3. Use your pattern to figure out how many unshaded triangles are in Stage Ten of Sierpinski's Triangle. _____

4. Find a formula for finding the number of unshaded triangles there are in Stage *n* of Sierpinski's Triangle.

_____

_____

_____

5. How can you find out the number of *shaded* triangles in Stage Ten of Sierpinski's Triangle?

_____

_____

_____

On today's activity: (Circle one) ➤ I need to know more. ➤ I got it.

18 **Name** _____ **Date** _____

Get Started

1.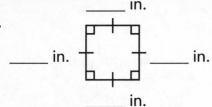

_____ in.

_____ in.

_____ in.

_____ in.

Perimeter = 64 inches

2.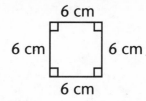

6 cm

6 cm   6 cm

6 cm

Perimeter = _____ centimeters

Go Further

3. Solve this riddle.

   Clues: • I am a parallelogram.

   • I have a perimeter equal to the number of inches in $2\frac{1}{2}$ yards.

   • I have two sides whose lengths are multiples of two, three, four, and six.

   • I have two sides whose lengths are multiples of three and eleven.

   What is the length of each of my sides? _____ inches

4. Fill in the blanks to make a Quadrilateral Perimeter Riddle.

   Clues: • I am a _____.

   • I have perimeter equal to _____.

   • I have _____ whose lengths are multiples of _____.

   • I have _____ whose lengths are multiples of _____.

   What is the length of each of my sides? _____

5. Now write your own riddle for a friend to solve.

   Clues: _____

   _____

   _____

   What is the length of each of my sides? _____

   Friend's name _____

On today's activity: (Circle one) I need to know more. I got it.

Name

Date

Get Started Working backward is a very good way to solve problems in which you know what you have at the end of a process, but don't know what you started with.

Billy's grandfather gave him some money for his birthday. The first thing Billy did with the money was to buy a CD for $12.95. He then went to a movie that cost $6.00. While at the movie, he lost a nickel. He spent $\frac{1}{2}$ of the money he had left for a snack. He now has $5.50 left. How much money did Billy's grandfather give him?

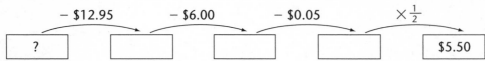

Today's Challenge Write your answer in the space provided.
Solve these problems by working backward.

1. On August 1, a car dealer decided to double the number of cars on her lot so that the dealership could have a big sale. That month the dealership sold 90 cars. The following month they sold 64 more. They then purchased 22 more cars so that they could have 150 cars on the lot. How many cars did they have at the beginning of August? _____

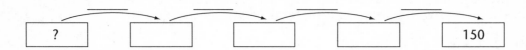

2. You need to get to school by 7 A.M. tomorrow for a special band practice. It takes five minutes to walk to the bus stop and $\frac{1}{2}$ hour for the bus ride to school. You usually spend 20 minutes getting cleaned-up and dressed, 15 minutes eating breakfast, and $\frac{1}{2}$ hour walking and feeding the dog. When should you get up tomorrow morning? _____

3. What advice would you give to a student who has the steps and the result but not the starting point of a problem?

_____

_____

_____

On today's activity: (Circle one) I need to know more. I got it.

20 **Name**

Date

Today's Challenge   Organize these terms into the correct categories.

1. These are words that describe types of angles.

   _____   _____

   _____   _____

   _____

2. These are words that name different quadrilaterals.

   _____   _____

   _____   _____

   _____

3. These are words that name polygons that are not quadrilaterals.

   _____   _____

   _____   _____

   _____

hexagon
parallelogram
acute
rhombus
trapezoid
octagon
rectangle
right
triangle
obtuse
square
pentagon

Go Further

4. Order these polygons by number of sides, from fewest to most.

   _____

   _____

   _____

   _____

rhombus
octagon
triangle
pentagon
hexagon
decagon

On today's activity: (Circle one)   I need to know more.   I got it.

Name   **Date**   **21**

Today's Challenge   Nines are Wild Challenge

Use the 1–9 digit cards to form three-digit addends. You are looking for three addends with a sum of 999. Each card will be used only once. Record your solutions here. Note: two solutions are *not* different if the three addends are switched: 123 + 456 + 789 is equivalent to 123 + 789 + 456.

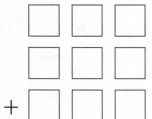
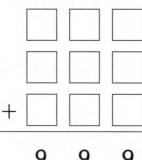
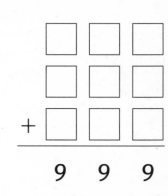

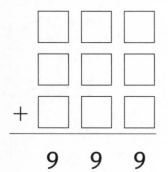
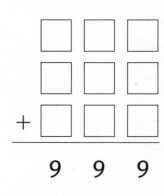

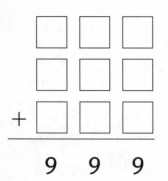
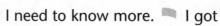

On today's activity: (Circle one)   I need to know more.   I got it.

Date

Go Further Nines are Wild Challenge

You have found several solutions to the Nines are Wild Challenge. Work with a partner and look at the solutions you have to the problem. Some of your solutions may be similar. Try to discover anything that is true about all of the solutions.

Things we discovered: _____

_____

_____

_____

_____

You can find new solutions by looking at other solutions. By switching the numbers in the ones place in each addend, you can generate new solutions. In fact, there are six solutions that can be found by switching the ones in the three addends. You could also generate six new solutions by switching the tens digits around. By switching the ones and tens digits around you can generate 6 × 6 or 36 solutions.

1. Take one of your solutions and generate all 36 members of that family of solutions.

2. What else might you do to generate new solutions?

_____

_____

On today's activity: (Circle one) I need to know more. I got it.

Name   **Date**   23

Get Started

	1 Gallon	1 Quart	1 Pint
	16 cups	4 cups	2 cups
	8 pints	2 pints	
	4 quarts		

Today's Challenge — Fill in the table.

Gallons	Quarts	Pints	Cups
1 gallon	4 quarts	8 pints	16 cups
1. $\frac{1}{2}$ gallon	_____	_____	8 cups
2. _____	1 quart	2 pints	_____
3. _____	_____	6 pints	12 cups
4. $2\frac{1}{2}$ gallons	_____	_____	_____

On today's activity: (Circle one) — I need to know more. — I got it.

 24 Name

Date

Get Started

Tell which fraction is greater and how you know. Use zero, one half, and one as benchmarks to help you explain your reasoning.

(A) $\frac{3}{7}$ or $\frac{2}{7}$ _____

(B) $\frac{3}{5}$ or $\frac{4}{9}$ _____

(C) $\frac{3}{4}$ or $\frac{5}{6}$ _____

(D) $\frac{5}{7}$ or $\frac{5}{8}$ _____

Today's Challenge   Fill in the circle of the correct answer. Use zero, one half, and one as benchmarks to help you explain your reasoning on the lines provided.

1. Which fraction is greater?

   (A) $\frac{12}{13}$ _____

   (B) $\frac{6}{7}$ _____

2. Which fraction is greater?

   (A) $\frac{5}{9}$ _____

   (B) $\frac{5}{8}$ _____

3. Which fraction is greater?

   (A) $\frac{1}{3}$ _____

   (B) $\frac{2}{9}$ _____

4. Which fraction is greater?

   (A) $\frac{3}{4}$ _____

   (B) $\frac{7}{6}$ _____

5. Which fraction is greater?

   (A) $\frac{9}{20}$ _____

   (B) $\frac{6}{11}$ _____

6. Which fraction is less?

   (A) $\frac{7}{8}$ _____

   (B) $\frac{3}{4}$ _____

7. Which fraction is less?

   (A) $\frac{7}{8}$ _____

   (B) $\frac{3}{5}$ _____

8. Which fraction is less?

   (A) $\frac{1}{3}$ _____

   (B) $\frac{1}{2}$ _____

9. What advice would you give to a student taking a test on comparing or ordering fractions?

   _____

   _____

   _____

   _____

On today's activity: (Circle one)   I need to know more.   I got it.

Name _____   **Date** _____   25

Today's Challenge — Fill in the blanks in this table to show decimals and fractions that are equivalent. Write fractions in simplest form.

	Decimal	Fraction
1.	0.8	
2.		$\frac{3}{4}$
3.	0.5	
4.		$\frac{1}{4}$
5.		$\frac{2}{5}$
6.	0.1	
7.		$\frac{1}{5}$
8.	0.6	
9.		$\frac{1}{8}$
10.	0.375	

Go Further

11. Write these fractions and decimals in order from least to greatest.

0.3		$\frac{2}{3}$
	$\frac{3}{4}$	
$\frac{2}{5}$		0.8
	$\frac{1}{8}$	
0.1		0.5
	$\frac{5}{6}$	

On today's activity: (Circle one) — I need to know more. — I got it.

Today's Challenge   Diagonals in a Polygon Challenge

A diagonal of a polygon is a line segment that connects two vertices, but it is not a side of the polygon. A triangle does not have any diagonals, and a quadrilateral has two. Use the polygons provided. Record in the table the number of diagonals at each vertex and the total number of diagonals in each polygon.

Polygon	Number of Diagonals at Each Vertex	Total Number of Diagonals

On today's activity: (Circle one)   I need to know more.   I got it.

Name   **Date**   27

Go Further — Diagonals in a Polygon Challenge

Work with a partner and see if you agree on the number of diagonals from each vertex of a polygon and the total number of diagonals for each polygon. Once you agree, fill in the table.

1. Study the table and try to discover patterns relating the number of sides for a polygon, the number of diagonals from a vertex for that polygon, and the total number of diagonals for that polygon.

Polygon	Number of Vertices (n)	Diagonals from Each Vertex (d)	nd	Total Number of Diagonals (D)
Triangle	3	0	$3 \times 0 = 0$	0
Quadrilateral				
Pentagon				
Hexagon				
Heptagon				
Octagon				

Things we discovered:

2. What is the relationship between the number of diagonals from a vertex of a polygon and the number of vertices in that polygon?

_____

3. What is the relationship between the product nd and the total number of diagonals in the polygon?

_____

4. Using the information you just discovered, find the number of diagonals in a 20-sided polygon.

$n = $ _____ $d = $ _____ $nd = $ _____ total number of diagonals = _____

5. If you represented the number of vertices (or sides) of the polygon as n, how would you represent the number of diagonals from that vertex? _____

6. If D represents the number of diagonals in a polygon with n vertices, write a formula for the number of diagonals in that polygon. _____

On today's activity: (Circle one) — I need to know more. — I got it.

Date

Today's Challenge Find strings of four digits that can be used to write addition expressions with values that are greater than 0.75 but less than 1.25. You must supply the zeroes in the ones places and the decimal points. Write each expression and its value.

4	6	2	8
3	5	6	7
5	7	3	2
4	1	6	3

_____

_____

_____

_____

Go Further **Create your own Math Jumble.** Include at least five addition expressions with values that are greater than 0.75 but less than 1.25. Have a friend find these expressions in your Math Jumble. Your friend must supply the zeroes in the ones places and the decimal points. Have your friend write each expression and its value. If you disagree on the expressions or their values, go back and check your work. Edit if necessary.

_____

_____

_____

_____

_____

Friend's name _____

On today's activity: (Circle one) I need to know more. I got it.

Name   **Date**   29

Ace the Test

Get Started Complete the constructed response.

Problem: Find at least three different fractions between $\frac{1}{4}$ and $\frac{1}{2}$.

Solution: *Between* $\frac{1}{4}$ and $\frac{1}{2}$ means greater than $\frac{1}{4}$ and less than $\frac{1}{2}$. Draw a number line.

Equally divide the number line in different ways and look for solutions.

Write a clear, complete answer to the problem.

A. _____ are three fractions

between **B.** _____.

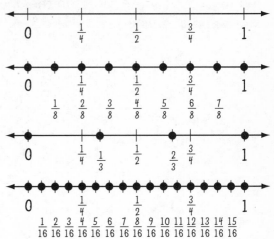

Today's Challenge Construct a clear, complete response. Be sure to show and explain all of your work.

1. **Problem:** Find a number between 200 and 300 that follows these rules.
   • It is odd.
   • It is a multiple of five.
   • The sum of its digits is 12.
   Solution: (Be sure to explain how you followed every rule.)

   _____

   _____

   _____

   _____

   _____

   _____

   _____

   _____

2. What advice would you give to someone taking his or her first constructed response test?

   _____

   _____

On today's activity: (Circle one) I need to know more. I got it.

Date

Today's Challenge — Show how much more you would need.

1. How much more lemon juice do I need for my recipe? I poured in one cup and I need one quart. _____

2. When will my cake be done? I put it in at 2:25 P.M. and it needs to bake for three fourths of an hour. _____

3. How much more wire do I need? I have $1\frac{1}{3}$ yards, but I need $6\frac{1}{3}$ yards. _____

4. You have driven at 60 miles per hour for two hours. At the same rate, about how much more time must you keep driving if you need to go 150 miles? _____

5. How much longer is the airplane flight? It is now 9:12 A.M. and the plane lands at 11:02 A.M. (It doesn't change time zones.) _____

6. How much more money do I need to buy a music CD? It costs $15.95 and I have saved $12.30. _____

7. I have added four fluid ounces of milk to the recipe. How much more must I add if the recipe calls for two cups? _____

8. How much change should I give a customer who paid for a $4.26 purchase with a $20.00 bill? _____

9. How much longer will I have to wait for a movie that starts at 7:30 P.M. if it is 4:45 P.M. right now? _____

10. I have six dollars, eight quarters, two dimes, and one nickel. I want to buy a movie poster for $13.98. How much more do I need? _____

Go Further — Show your work on another piece of paper.

11. How long it is from 8:30 in the morning until 2:15 in the afternoon. Show and explain your work.

12. Find the number of hours and minutes it took to finish your project. Show and explain your work.

Day	Time Spent on Project
Monday (start)	$2\frac{1}{4}$ hours
Tuesday	$3\frac{2}{3}$ hours
Wednesday	2 hours, 25 minutes
Thursday	1 hour, 35 minutes
Friday (finish)	4 hours, 50 minutes

On today's activity: (Circle one)　I need to know more.　I got it.

Name _____　Date _____　31

Today's Challenge Three-Digit Product Challenge.

Use the 4–9 digit cards to form two 3-digit numbers whose product is very large. Keep trying new combinations until you think you have found the greatest possible product. You can use each digit only once. Record your work here.

☐ ☐ ☐   ☐ ☐ ☐   ☐ ☐ ☐
× ☐ ☐ ☐   × ☐ ☐ ☐   × ☐ ☐ ☐
_____   _____   _____

☐ ☐ ☐   ☐ ☐ ☐   ☐ ☐ ☐
× ☐ ☐ ☐   × ☐ ☐ ☐   × ☐ ☐ ☐
_____   _____   _____

☐ ☐ ☐   ☐ ☐ ☐   ☐ ☐ ☐
× ☐ ☐ ☐   × ☐ ☐ ☐   × ☐ ☐ ☐
_____   _____   _____

☐ ☐ ☐   ☐ ☐ ☐   ☐ ☐ ☐
× ☐ ☐ ☐   × ☐ ☐ ☐   × ☐ ☐ ☐
_____   _____   _____

On today's activity: (Circle one) I need to know more. I got it.

Name   **Date**

Go Further — **Three-Digit Product Challenge**

You have probably found the greatest possible product for this challenge. Work with a partner to describe any features of the factors which give the greatest product.

Things we discovered: _____

_____

_____

_____

Many times in mathematics, you can use what you learned from one problem to solve a related problem. In this case, what you learned about the greatest possible product of three-digit factors can help you with related challenges.

1. Arrange the digits 1–6 into three-digit factors with the *greatest* possible product. Explain your thinking.

_____

_____

_____

2. Arrange the digits 4–9 into three-digit factors with the *least* possible product. Explain your thinking.

_____

_____

_____

3. Arrange the digits 1–6 into three-digit factors with the *least* possible product. Explain your thinking.

_____

_____

_____

On today's activity: (Circle one) — I need to know more. — I got it.

Name

Date

33

Go Further 🖋 **Fill in the calendar, then follow the directions to mark dates.**
Some will be marked more than once.

1. Cross out all dates that are less than one week after May third.

2. Circle all dates that are more than one week before May seventeenth.

3. Star all dates that are multiples of six.

4. Box all dates that are on weekends.

5. Underline all dates that are composite numbers.

6. Which Monday is not marked?

   _____

MAY

S	M	T	W	Th	F	S
			1			

7. Create your own "Fantastic Finalist" activity for a friend to solve. If you disagree on the answer, recheck your work and edit if you need to.

   • _____

   • _____

   • _____

   • _____

   • _____

JULY

S	M	T	W	Th	F	S
	1					

Which _____ is not marked? _____

Friend's name _____

On today's activity: (Circle one) 🖋 I need to know more. 🖋 I got it.

Get Started Without factoring, decide which number is the greatest common factor for **126 and 270**. Explain your reasoning.

(A) 4 _____

(B) 9 _____

(C) 18 _____

(D) 3 _____

Today's Challenge Circle the letter of the correct answer.

Find the greatest common factor for each pair of numbers. Explain your reasoning.

1. 210 and 180
   (A) 4 _____
   (B) 10 _____
   (C) 15 _____
   (D) 30 _____

2. 195 and 231
   (A) 3 _____
   (B) 6 _____
   (C) 9 _____
   (D) 15 _____

3. 252 and 204
   (A) 12 _____
   (B) 6 _____
   (C) 18 _____
   (D) 4 _____

4. 25 and 6750
   (A) 9 _____
   (B) 5 _____
   (C) 10 _____
   (D) 25 _____

5. 72 and 1431
   (A) 2 _____
   (B) 9 _____
   (C) 3 _____
   (D) 11 _____

6. 25 and 729
   (A) 1 _____
   (B) 5 _____
   (C) 3 _____
   (D) 9 _____

7. What advice would you give to a student looking for greatest common factors on a test?

_____

_____

_____

On today's activity: (Circle one) I need to know more. I got it.

Name _____ Date _____ 35

Today's Challenge Find the least common multiple for each pair of numbers.

Think: multiples of 12: 12, 24, 36, 48, 60, 72, 84, 96 } The least common multiple of 12 and 15 is 60.

multiples of 15: 15, 30, 45, 60

Think: multiples of 4: 4, 8 } The least common multiple of 4 and 8 is 8.

multiples of 8: 8

1. Find the least common multiple of 7 and 4. _____

2. Find the least common multiple of 10 and 15. _____

3. Find the least common multiple of 6 and 12. _____

4. Find the least common multiple of 4 and 5. _____

5. Find the least common multiple of 8 and 12. _____

6. Find the least common multiple of 8 and 3. _____

7. Find the least common multiple of 9 and 6. _____

8. Find the least common multiple of 15 and 9. _____

9. Find the least common multiple of 12 and 10. _____

10. Find the least common multiple of 9 and 36. _____

Go Further Write the exercise number (1–10) in the box that describes the answer to that exercise.

11. If the numbers are a and b, the least common multiple is either a or b.	12. If the numbers are a and b, then the least common multiple is $a \times b$.	13. The least common multiple is not described by exercise 12 or 13.

14. Tell when you think the least common multiple will be the product of the two numbers.

On today's activity: (Circle one) I need to know more. I got it.

Date

Today's Challenge   Solving *Magic* Mathematics Problems

Here is a problem with many different answers. How will you know
if you got it right? The answer indicates your age.

- Write your age. _____

- Multiply by five. _____

- Add six to the product. _____

- Multiply the sum by four. _____

- Add nine to the product. _____

- Multiply the sum by five. _____

- Subtract 165 from the product. _____

Do you see your age? You should. The first two digits of the answer
tell your age.

How does this problem work so that you always get your age as part of the
answer? Study the directions and the step-by-step calculations you did.
Explain why anyone who follows these directions always ends up with his or
her age followed by two zeros.

_____

_____

_____

_____

_____

_____

_____

_____

_____

On today's activity: (Circle one)   I need to know more.   I got it.

Name

Date

Go Further — Solving *Magic* Mathematics Problems

Work with a friend to analyze the age problem.

Things we discovered: _____

_____

_____

_____

1. How can you undo multiplying by six or subtracting five?

   _____

   _____

2. If you add five to a number and then double the sum, what must you do to undo these two steps?

   _____

   _____

3. Is adding five to a number and then doubling the number the same as first doubling and then adding five? Explain.

   _____

   _____

4. Use the age problem as a model to make up your own problem. Try it out on a friend. Edit your work if necessary.

   _____

   _____

   _____

   _____

   _____

On today's activity: (Circle one)   I need to know more.   I got it.

Name _____

Date _____

Get Started For each question, write *yes* or *no*.

1. Is 75 a multiple of 9? _____

2. Is 75 an even number? _____

3. Is the sum of the digits in 75 evenly divisible by three? _____

4. Is 75 a prime number? _____

5. Is 59 an even number? _____

6. Is 59 a multiple of five or ten? _____

7. Is the sum of the digits in 59 evenly divisible by three? _____

8. Is 59 a prime number? _____

Go Further

9. Solve this riddle.

   Clues: • I am a prime number.

   • I am greater than 50 but less than 70.

   • I am between multiples of ten and the next multiple of nine.

   • I do not have a multiple of three in my ones place.

   What number am I? _____

10. Now write your own riddle for a friend to solve.

   Clues: _____

   _____

   _____

   _____

   What number am I? _____

   Friend's name _____

On today's activity: (Circle one) I need to know more. I got it.

Name   **Date**

Get Started ✐ Fill in the circle of the correct answer.

Aileen was taking a test. Here are four examples of Aileen's work. Mark the letter of each problem that Aileen has solved correctly, then correct her mistakes.

(A) 54.5
    − 16.8
     42.3
  _____

(B)   8.24
    − 3.65
      5.41
  _____

(C)   659
    − 129
      530
  _____

(D)   43.4
    − 24.2
      21.2
  _____

Today's Challenge ✐ Fill in the circle of the correct answer.

Which of these exercises do you think Aileen would do correctly?

1. (A)   465   (B)   4.75   (C)   65.9   (D)   86.4
        − 123   − 3.96   − 12.1   − 39.6

2. (A) 7.65   (B)   625   (C)   36.4   (D)   38.6
        − 4.87   − 537   − 18.5   − 12.4

Choose the letter that shows the correct answer, followed by the answer you think Aileen would give.

3. 625 − 476
    (A) 149; 251
    (B) 251; 249
    (C) 149; 249
    (D) 251; Aileen would answer correctly.

4. 15.5 − 3.2
    (A) 12.3; 7.7
    (B) 12.3; 1.77
    (C) 123; 1.77
    (D) 12.3; Aileen would answer correctly.

If Aileen cannot do the example, mark the letter of the related example she *can* do.

5. 824 − 136
    (A) 832 − 126
    (B) 836 − 124
    (C) 136 − 824
    (D) No change needed.

6. 4.56 − 2.68
    (A) 4.58 − 2.66
    (B) 2.56 − 4.68
    (C) 4.68 − 2.56
    (D) No change needed.

7. What advice would you give Aileen about subtracting decimals?

    _____

    _____

On today's activity: (Circle one) ✐ I need to know more. ✐ I got it.

40   Name

Date

Today's Challenge Find the value of each expression.

1. What is the value of $5x + 3$ if $x = 4$? _____

2. What is the value of $x + 9$ if $x = 2$? _____

3. What is the value of $2x - 1$ if $x = 5$? _____

4. What is the value of $4 + 2x$ if $x = 7$? _____

5. What is the value of $4 + x^2$ if $x = 3$? _____

6. What is the value of $4x \div 4$ if $x = 1$? _____

7. What is the value of $3(x - 3)$ if $x = 8$? _____

8. What is the value of $8 + 4x$ if $x = 6$? _____

9. What is the value of $x^2 - 21$ if $x = 9$? _____

10. What is the value of $17 - 3x$ if $x = 5$? _____

Go Further

11. Find the value of the expression $2x + 3$ when the value for x changes.
Record your answers in the table.

Expression	Value of x	Answer
$2x + 3$	3	
$2x + 3$	4	
$2x + 3$	5	
$2x + 3$	6	

12. What pattern do you notice in your answers? Explain.

_____

_____

On today's activity: (Circle one)   I need to know more.   I got it.

Name   **Date**

Today's Challenge ✏ Use Logic to Cross a River

You have a fox, a goose, and a bag of corn and you need to cross a river. The boat you need to use will hold only you and one other item: the corn, the goose, or the fox. Unfortunately, if you leave the fox alone with the goose, the fox will eat the goose. If you leave the goose alone with the corn, the goose will eat the corn.

You can cross the river with the boat as often as you want. You may use colored squares to keep track as you work out the problem. Draw a diagram and describe your steps for safely moving the corn, the fox, and the goose to the other side of the river.

On today's activity: (Circle one) ✏ I need to know more. ✏ I got it.

Name

Date

Go Further Use Logic to Cross a River

Work with a friend. Use the questions to help you analyze your solution and the way you worked it out.

Things we discovered:

1. What ideas helped you solve the problem?

_____

_____

_____

2. How did the colored squares help you solve the problem?

_____

_____

_____

Now you have the fox, goose, and corn plus some fishing worms. Worms eat corn and geese eat worms.

3. Draw a diagram to illustrate a way to get everything across the river if your boat holds you and *two* other items.

_____

_____

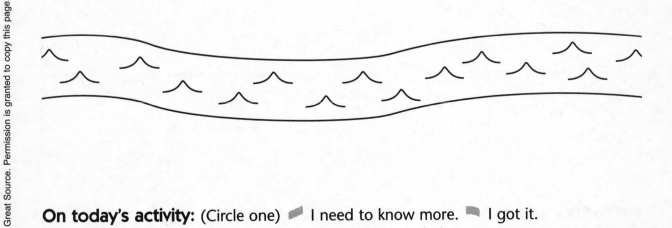

On today's activity: (Circle one) I need to know more. I got it.

Name **Date** 43

Get Started

Example 1

Fraction	Decimal
$\frac{3}{4}$	<u>0.75</u>

Example 2

Fraction	Decimal
$\frac{3}{5}$	0.6

Today's Challenge   Complete the table. Simplify fractions.

	Fraction	Decimal		Fraction	Decimal
1.	$\frac{1}{2}$	_____	2.	$\frac{4}{5}$	_____
3.	_____	0.1	4.	$\frac{3}{10}$	_____
5.	$\frac{1}{8}$	_____	6.	_____	0.9
7.	_____	0.2	8.	_____	0.25
9.	_____	0.7	10.	$\frac{2}{5}$	_____

On today's activity: (Circle one)   I need to know more.   I got it.

44 Name

Date

Get Started

Barb Wire was taking a test. Here are four examples of Barb's work.
Mark the letter of each problem that Barb has solved correctly, then correct her mistakes.

A. Round to the nearest tenth: 0.45 → ___0.4_____

B. Round to the nearest hundredth: 1.235 → ___1.23_____

C. Round to the nearest tenth: 0.53 → ___0.5_____

D. Round to the nearest hundredth: 3.3466 → ___3.35_____

Today's Challenge Mark the letter of any correct answer. Write explanations for your choices on the lines provided.

1. Which of these exercises do you think Barb would do correctly?

A. Round to the nearest tenth: 0.65 _____

B. Round to the nearest hundredth: 2.345 _____

C. Round to the nearest tenth: 2.751 _____

D. Round to the nearest hundredth: 4.763 _____

Rewrite these examples so that Barb can do them but the answers will match. Then round.

2. Round to the nearest tenth: 2.65 _____

3. Round to the nearest hundredth: 3.655 _____

4. Round to the nearest thousandth: 6.7885_____

5. What advice would you give Barb about rounding to a given place?

_____

_____

_____

_____

_____

_____

On today's activity: (Circle one) I need to know more. I got it.

Name _____ **Date** _____

Today's Challenge   Fill in this table by adding the fraction at the top of the column to the fraction at the left of the row.
Write your sum in simplest form.

+	$\frac{1}{2}$	$\frac{1}{3}$	$\frac{3}{4}$	$\frac{5}{6}$
1. $\frac{1}{4}$				
2. $\frac{2}{3}$				
3. $\frac{5}{6}$				

Go Further

4. Write the sums in the table above in order from least to greatest.

_____

_____

5. Make your own fraction-addition table for a friend to solve. Write your answers on another piece of paper.

Friend's name

_____

On today's activity: (Circle one)   I need to know more.   I got it.

Date

Today's Challenge — Perfect Number Challenge

When the factors of a number (except the number itself) have a sum equal to the number, that number is *perfect*. If this sum is less than the number, the number is *deficient*. If the sum is greater than the number, the number is *abundant*.

Six is perfect.
- Its factors are 1, 2, 3, and 6.
- $1 + 2 + 3 = 6$, so six is perfect.

Nine is not perfect.
- Its factors are 1, 3, and 9.
- $1 + 3 < 9$, so nine is deficient.

Twelve is not perfect.
- Its factors are 1, 2, 3, 4, 6, and 12.
- $1 + 2 + 3 + 4 + 6 > 12$, so twelve is abundant.

There are only two perfect numbers less than 100. As you look for the second perfect number, list the numbers you check in the appropriate column of the table.

Number	Factors (except number)	Deficient?	Abundant?	Perfect?
6	1, 2, 3			✔
9	1, 3	✔		
12	1, 2, 3, 4, 6		✔	

On today's activity: (Circle one) — I need to know more. — I got it.

Name   Date   **47**

Go Further — Perfect Number Challenge

You have found two perfect numbers less than 100. Work with a partner to check and analyze your lists of abundant, deficient, and perfect numbers less than 100. Write what you notice about the numbers in each category.

Things we discovered: _____

_____

_____

_____

_____

_____

1. Why is it impossible for a prime number to be a perfect number?

   _____

   _____

   _____

2. What other group(s) of numbers cannot be perfect numbers?

   _____

   _____

   _____

   _____

   _____

3. The next perfect number is between 400 and 500. Use what you learned about perfect numbers to find the next largest perfect number.

   _____

On today's activity: (Circle one) — I need to know more. — I got it.

48 **Name**

Date

Today's Challenge Look for strings of two or three digits that form pairs of factors for the numbers in the table. Fill in the table with each pair you find.

Number	Factor pairs
24	_____
27	_____
36	_____
42	_____
45	_____
48	_____

8	1	6	6
9	2	2	7
4	8	3	1
5	9	3	4

Go Further

1. List all of the factors of 24. _____

2. List all of the factors of 36. _____

3. List all of the factors of 48. _____

4. What are the common factors of 24 and 36? _____

5. What is the greatest common factor of 24 and 36? _____

6. What is the greatest common factor of 36 and 48? _____

7. What is the greatest common factor of 24 and 48? _____

8. What is the greatest common factor of 24, 36, and 48? _____

On today's activity: (Circle one) ◢ I need to know more. ◥ I got it.

Name _____ **Date** _____

Ace the Test

Get Started

Miles Away was taking a test. Here are four examples of his work. Mark the letter of each expression that Miles has evaluated correctly.

Ⓐ $3 \times 4 + 6 =$ __18__   Ⓑ $6 \times 4 + 3 \times 2 =$ __54__

Ⓒ $45 \div 3 - 5 \times 3 + 8 =$ __38__   Ⓓ $45 \div 15 + 6 - 2 =$ __7__

Today's Challenge

1. Which of these expressions do you think Miles would evaluate correctly? Explain, then write the value of each expression.

   Ⓐ $7 \times 8 - 4 \times 2$ _____   Ⓑ $6 \times 3 - 4$ _____

   Ⓒ $4 + 9 \div 3 + 20$ _____   Ⓓ $8 - 3 \times 2$ _____

Revise these expressions so that Miles can evaluate them correctly. Explain your adjustments, then write the correct answer. The first is done for you.

2. $3 + 4 \times 5$ __Miles would add first, then multiply. To make him multiply first, change the__ __order: 4 X 5 + 3 = 23 or put in some parentheses: 3 + (4 X 5) = 23.__

3. $8 + 6 \div 2 - 5$ _____

_____

4. $9 \times 4 + 3$ _____

_____

5. $6 \times 10 + 8 \div 2$ _____

_____

6. $6 + 12 \div 3$ _____

_____

7. $9 + 4 \times 3 - 7 \times 2$ _____

_____

8. What advice would you give Miles about problems containing more than one operation?

_____

_____

On today's activity: (Circle one) ✎ I need to know more. ✎ I got it.

50 Name

Date

Today's Challenge 📎 **Find these mystery numbers.**

1. What is 20,000 less than 154,012? _____

2. What is 10^2 less than 134,099? _____

3. What is $(9 \times 10^3) + (6 \times 10^2) + 5$? _____

4. What is 10^4 less than 100,000? _____

5. What is $803,906 + (8 \times 10^4)$? _____

6. What is 10^2 less than 134,299? _____

7. What is (9×10^2) less than 134,999? _____

8. What is 10^2 greater than 914? _____

9. What is 10^2 less than 9,645,032? _____

10. What is 10^2 more than 7904? _____

Go Further

11. Write the answers to exercises 1–10 in order from least to greatest.

_____

12. Write four of your own *Mystery Number* exercises. All four should have the same answer. Share your problems with a friend, then check that your answers agree.

_____

_____

_____

_____

_____

Friend's name _____

On today's activity: (Circle one) 📎 I need to know more. 📎 I got it.

Name _____ **Date** _____ **51**

Today's Challenge ☞ Arranging Five Squares

How many different ways can you arrange two squares on a plane? Not many if they have to share a full side. There is only one way, put them next to each other. What about three squares? There are only two different ways to arrange three squares.

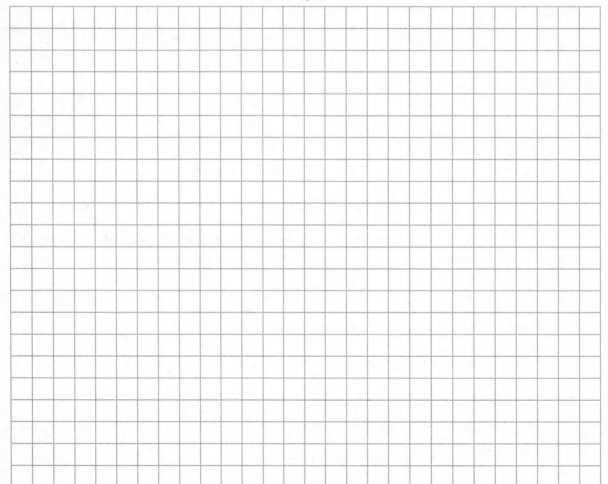

Two Squares   **Three Squares**

Notice that each square shares a whole side with at least one other square. How many different ways can you arrange five squares? Use the colored squares to help decide. Every time you find a new arrangement, record it in the box. A rotation or reflection is *not* a new arrangement.

Five Squares

On today's activity: (Circle one) ☞ I need to know more. ☞ I got it.

Date

Go Further — Arranging Five Squares

Did you get all 12 possible arrangements of five squares? Work with a partner to study your answers for activity 52.

Things we discovered:

1. If you had any duplicates, how do they look different? What can you do to prevent duplicates?

   _____

   _____

2. How can you make an organized search for arrangements like these?

   _____

   _____

3. Which of your arrangements can be folded into a box without a top? Draw them here.

4. Use what you learned and follow the same rules to find all possible arrangements of four squares.

On today's activity: (Circle one) — I need to know more. — I got it.

Name   **Date**

Go Further — Follow the directions to mark fractions in the grid.

$\frac{2}{3}$	$\frac{6}{8}$	$\frac{2}{4}$	$\frac{3}{9}$
$\frac{6}{10}$	$\frac{1}{4}$	$\frac{2}{8}$	$\frac{4}{5}$
$\frac{3}{4}$	$\frac{2}{5}$	$\frac{4}{6}$	$\frac{8}{10}$
$\frac{1}{3}$	$\frac{4}{10}$	$\frac{3}{5}$	$\frac{1}{2}$

1. Cross out all fractions equal to $\frac{1}{5} + \frac{2}{5}$.

2. Circle all fractions equal to $\frac{2}{6} + \frac{2}{6}$.

3. Star all fractions equal to $\frac{1}{9} + \frac{2}{9}$.

4. Underline all fractions equal to $\frac{1}{4} + \frac{2}{4}$.

5. Box all fractions equal to $\frac{1}{8} + \frac{1}{8}$.

6. Shade squares containing fractions equal to $\frac{5}{10} + \frac{3}{10}$.

7. Draw a triangle around all fractions equal to $\frac{3}{10} + \frac{1}{10}$.

8. Which pair of equivalent fractions is not marked? _____

Write two expressions with values equal to these fractions.

Example $\frac{4}{5}$: _____ $\frac{2}{5} + \frac{2}{5}$; $\frac{1}{5} + \frac{3}{5}$ _____

9. $\frac{5}{7}$ _____

10. $\frac{7}{9}$ _____

On today's activity: (Circle one) — I need to know more. — I got it.

 54 **Name** _____

Date _____

Get Started

Patti was taking a test. Here are two examples of Patti's work. Mark the letter of each expression that Patti has rewritten correctly, then correct her mistakes.

A. $2(x - 3) = $ _____ $2x - 6$ _____ **B.** $4x + 8 = $ _____ $4(x + 8)$ _____

Today's Challenge   Mark the letter of the correct answer.

Explain each choice on the lines provided.

1. Which of these expressions do you think Patti would rewrite correctly? Explain, then simplify each.

   A. $4(x + 4)$ _____

   B. $6x + 42$ _____

   C. $8(x - 3)$ _____

Choose the factor that will best help you use the Distributive Property to rewrite the expression.

2. $4x - 2$	3. $25x + 5xy$	4. $\frac{x}{2} + 8$	5. $27x - 18y$
A. 4	A. 5	A. 2	A. 9
B. 2	B. $5x$	B. 8	B. 1
C. x	C. x	C. $\frac{1}{2}$	C. 27

6. $72x + 5$	7. $128x + 14$	8. $\frac{5x}{6} - 30$	9. $\frac{6x}{3} + 18$
A. x	A. 2	A. 5	A. 2
B. 5	B. 7	B. 6	B. 3
C. None of these.	C. None of these.	C. None of these.	C. None of these.

10. What advice would you give Patti about solving problems using the Distributive Property?

   _____

   _____

   _____

   _____

On today's activity: (Circle one)   I need to know more.   I got it.

Name _____ **Date** _____

Today's Challenge

1. If $x - 13 = 4$, what is x? _____
2. If $x + 9 = 28$, what is x? _____
3. If $9x = 54$, what is x? _____
4. If $21 + x = 64$ what is x? _____
5. If $x \div 12 = 6$, what is x? _____
6. If $2x + 8 = 16$, what is x? _____
7. If $x^2 = 121$, what is x? _____
8. If $12x = 96$, what is x? _____
9. If $5x - 20 = 25$, what is x? _____
10. If $10x + 35 = 145$, what is x? _____

Go Further Write the questions for these answers. Then, share your questions with a friend.

Example

If the answer is $x = 5$, you could write

$5x = 25$, $x = ?$ or

$25 \div x = 5$, $x = ?$ or

$x + 3 = 8$, $x = ?$ or

$12 - x = 7$, $x = ?$ or

$4(x + 2) = 28$, $x = ?$, or . . .

11. Answer: $x = 7$ Question: _____
12. Answer: $x = 10$ Question: _____
13. Answer: $x = 13$ Question: _____
14. Answer: $x = 21$ Question: _____
15. Answer: $x = 100$ Question: _____

Friend's name _____

On today's activity: (Circle one)   I need to know more.   I got it.

Today's Challenge ✏ Making Magic Squares

In a magic square, the numbers in the rows, columns, and diagonals must have the same sum. Can you make two different magic squares in the grid shown here? Fill in numbers 1–9 to make each magic square. Remember you can use each number once in each grid.

On today's activity: (Circle one) ✏ I need to know more. ▪ I got it.

Name   **Date**

Go Further Making Magic Squares

Work with a friend to compare magic squares.

Things we discovered: _____

_____

_____

_____

_____

Many times in mathematics you can use one solution as a model for more solutions. This is true for magic squares.

1. How can you make a new magic square from an existing one?

   _____

   _____

2. How can you change all of the numbers in a magic square and still have a magic square? *Hint*: You won't be using 1–9 in your new square.

   _____

   _____

   _____

3. Use the equality properties to help you make up at least two more magic squares. One of your magic squares should have the number 16 in it. Be sure to explain how you changed the original magic square to make your new ones.

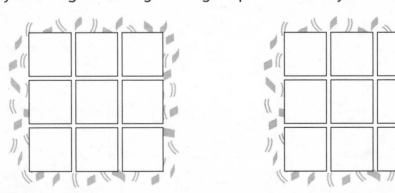

On today's activity: (Circle one) I need to know more. I got it.

Date

Get Started

1. Complete the table.

Word Name	Fraction Form	Decimal Form	Percent Form
three fourths			
one tenth			
three fifths			
one fourth			
one fifth			

Go Further — Solve the riddles.

2. **Clues:** • I can be written as a decimal with its only non-zero digit in the tenths place.
   • I am less than one half.
   • I am greater than 15% but less than 25%.

   What is my fraction name? _____

3. **Clues:** • I can be written as a fraction with three as the numerator.
   • I am greater than one half.
   • I am less than 0.7.

   What is my percent name? _____

4. Now write your own riddle for a friend to solve.

   Clues: _____

   _____

   _____

   What is my decimal name? _____

   Friend's name _____

On today's activity: (Circle one) — I need to know more. — I got it.

Get Started Tessa was taking a test. Here are four examples of Tessa's work. Mark the letter of each expression that Tessa has evaluated correctly.

A. 0.4 + 1.23 + 5.3 = _____1.80_____

B. 1.8 + 0.6 + 0.4 = _____2.8_____

C. 3.6 + 0.42 + 5.1 = _____1.29_____

D. 4.3 + 8.73 + 4.26 = _____13.42_____

Today's Challenge

1. Which of these expressions do you think Tessa would evaluate correctly? Explain.

   A. 6.32 + 0.5 + 3.36 _____

   B. 3.43 + 5.63 + 4.32 _____

   C. 4.3 + 7.63 + 8.74 _____

   D. 4.66 + 9.34 + 7.6 _____

Use zeros as placeholders and rewrite these expressions so that Tessa can evaluate them correctly, then write the sums.

2. 5.6 + 5.32 + 8.45

   _____

3. 5.89 + 7.5 + 9.88

   _____

4. 3.1 + 0.73 + 2.4

   _____

5. 1.32 + 7.7 + 8.45

   _____

6. 4.5 + 8.3 + 8.53

   _____

7. 9.88 + 7.72 + 3.1

   _____

8. 2.25 + 4.3 + 8.2

   _____

9. 0.01 + 5.88 + 7.2

   _____

10. What advice would you give Tessa about adding decimals?

    _____

    _____

On today's activity: (Circle one) ✏ I need to know more. ✏ I got it.

Today's Challenge Fill in the blanks in this table to show the percent equivalent to the decimal or fraction value that is given.

	Given Value	Equivalent Percent
1.	$\frac{4}{5}$	
2.	0.75	
3.	$\frac{1}{2}$	
4.	0.25	
5.	0.4	
6.	$\frac{1}{10}$	
7.	0.2	
8.	$\frac{3}{5}$	
9.	0.65	
10.	$\frac{11}{20}$	

Go Further

11. Write these fractions, decimals, and percents in order from least to greatest.

50%	0.65
$\frac{3}{4}$	
40%	0.3
$\frac{2}{3}$	
85%	0.6
$\frac{9}{10}$	

On today's activity: (Circle one) I need to know more. I got it.

Name **Date** 61

Today's Challenge 〜 To Repeat or Not To Repeat

When a fraction is written as a decimal equivalent, the decimal equivalent does one of two things. It either terminates (for example, $\frac{3}{4} = 0.75$) or it repeats (for example, $\frac{1}{6} = 0.1\overline{6}$). You will be searching for a way to decide which repeat and which terminate. Fill in the table.

	Fraction	Terminating	Repeating	Prime Factorization of Denominator (ignore one)
1.	$\frac{1}{2}$	0.5		2
2.	$\frac{2}{3}$			
3.	$\frac{1}{4}$			
4.	$\frac{3}{5}$			
5.	$\frac{1}{6}$			
6.	$\frac{4}{7}$			
7.	$\frac{3}{8}$			
8.	$\frac{1}{9}$			
9.	$\frac{7}{10}$			
10.	$\frac{5}{11}$			
11.	$\frac{7}{12}$			
12.	$\frac{6}{13}$			
13.	$\frac{9}{12}$			
14.	$\frac{6}{15}$			
15.	$\frac{7}{28}$			
16.	$\frac{2}{9}$			
17.	$\frac{5}{12}$			
18.	$\frac{1}{7}$			
19.	$\frac{5}{13}$			
20.	$\frac{3}{9}$			

On today's activity: (Circle one) 〜 I need to know more. 〜 I got it.

Name

Date

Go Further — To Repeat or Not To Repeat

Look at your work on page 62. Work with a partner to see whether your answers agree. Once you have agreed, study the table for patterns and relationships.

Things we discovered:

1. What relationship do you see between the prime factors of the denominators and the form of the decimal?

   _____

   _____

   _____

2. Write a rule that helps you predict whether the decimal equivalent will repeat. Write your rule and your predictions here.

   _____

   _____

   _____

3. Now check your work by computing equivalent decimals for eight new fractions. Revise your rule if you need to.

   _____

   _____

   _____

4. Test your rule by stating whether these fractions will terminate when written as decimals.

   A. $\frac{4}{9}$ _____   B. $\frac{15}{24}$ _____   C. $\frac{7}{16}$ _____

   D. $\frac{8}{25}$ _____   E. $\frac{7}{22}$ _____

On today's activity: (Circle one) — I need to know more. — I got it.

Name _____   **Date** _____   63

Today's Challenge Evaluate each expression for the given value of *x*.

1. If *x* = 4, then
   3*x* + 5 = ?   _____

2. If *x* = 3, then
   x + *x* = ?   _____

3. If *x* = 7, then
   4*x* − 15 = ?   _____

4. If *x* = 4, then
   2(*x* + 3) = ?   _____

5. If *x* = 9, then
   3 + 2*x* = ?   _____

6. If *x* = 2, then
   3(*x* + 4) = ?   _____

7. If *x* = 6, then
   2*x* + 1 = ?   _____

8. If *x* = 2, then
   6*x* − 7 = ?   _____

9. If *x* = 2, then
   2(*x* + 1) = ?   _____

10. If *x* = 7, then
    4 + 3*x* = ?   _____

11. If *x* = 8, then
    7 + *x* = ?   _____

12. If *x* = 2, then
    9*x* − 1 = ?   _____

13. If *x* = 4, then
    5*x* − 6 = ?   _____

14. If *x* = 10, then
    x + 8 = ?   _____

15. If *x* = 4, then
    5(*x* + 1) = ?   _____

16. If *x* = 6, then
    4*x* − 3 = ?   _____

17. If *x* = 5, then
    x + 3*x* = ?   _____

18. If *x* = 8, then
    3*x* − 4 = ?   _____

19. If *x* = 5, then
    3*x* − 10 = ?   _____

20. If *x* = 4, then
    4*x* − 1 = ?   _____

On today's activity: (Circle one) I need to know more. I got it.

Name

Date

Get Started

Juan and Amanda were checking their answers to a homework exercise. Do not compute, but do study their work.

Amanda	Juan
18.25	18.25
× 5.34	× 5.34
9.7455	97.455

Who is correct? How could you tell? _____

_____

Today's Challenge ✐ **Circle the letter of the correct answer.** Without multiplying, choose the product that makes sense. Explain why you eliminated some answer choices and decided on the answer you did.

1. 13.6 × 8.32

   Ⓐ 1,131.52 _____

   Ⓑ 17.152 _____

   Ⓒ 113.152 _____

   Ⓓ 93.152 _____

2. 29.8 × 6.45

   Ⓐ 19.221 _____

   Ⓑ 192.21 _____

   Ⓒ 912.21 _____

   Ⓓ 391.221 _____

3. 94.82 × 6.35

   Ⓐ 602.107 _____

   Ⓑ 803.2064 _____

   Ⓒ 6021.07 _____

   Ⓓ 478.4023 _____

4. 23.8 × 8.95

   Ⓐ 21.301 _____

   Ⓑ 213.01 _____

   Ⓒ 2130.1 _____

   Ⓓ 308.12 _____

5. What advice would you give Amanda about multiplying decimal numbers?

   _____

   _____

   _____

On today's activity: (Circle one) ✐ I need to know more. ✐ I got it.

Name _____ **Date** _____ 65

Today's Challenge Choose your answers from this box. You won't use every number.

1. What is the only even prime number? _____

2. What is a composite number whose factors, other than one and itself, are seven and 11? _____

3. What is the greatest two-digit prime number? _____

4. What is the only counting number that is neither prime nor composite? _____

5. What is the greatest one-digit prime number? _____

6. What is the only odd number between 10 and 20 that is *not* prime? _____

7. Name the least number that is divisible by both four and six. _____

8. Find a two-digit prime number whose digits have a product that is prime. _____

9. Find a prime number between 30 and 40 whose digits have a sum of ten. _____

10. What is a multiple of six whose digits have a sum of 12? _____

15
1
77
9
2
3
7
97
48
18
13
99
12
0
37
29

Go Further

11. Cross out numbers that are not prime. Circle every prime number.

12. Describe a pattern in the numbers you have circled. *Hint*: The extra dark numbers are called the *multiples of six.*

_____

13. If the table were continued through 100, would your pattern continue? Explain.

_____

1	2	3	4	5	6
7	8	9	10	11	12
13	14	15	16	17	18
19	20	21	22	23	24
25	26	27	28	29	30
31	32	33	34	35	36
37	38	39	40	41	42
43	44	45	46	47	48
49	50	51	52	53	54
55	56	57	58	59	60

On today's activity: (Circle one) I need to know more. I got it.

Date

Today's Challenge — Garden Tiles

There is a flower garden surrounded by a walkway made of square tiles. Plants are arranged horizontally in one row, and the garden is always completely enclosed. The diagrams indicate flower gardens with one and two plants. On the grid, build flower gardens with three, four, five, and six plants. Record your results in the table.

Number of Plants	Number of Tiles
1	
2	
3	
4	
5	
6	

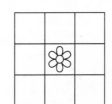 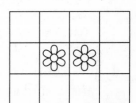

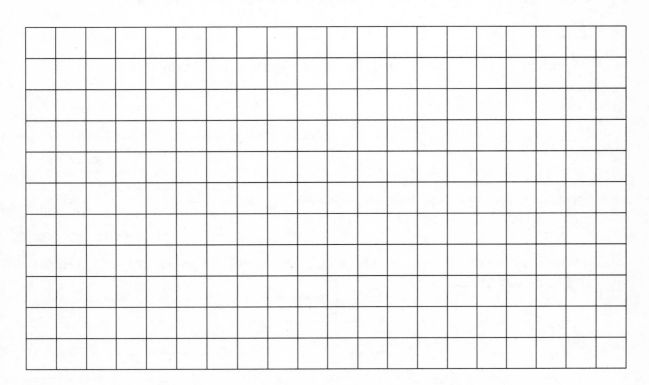

On today's activity: (Circle one) — I need to know more. — I got it.

Name **Date**

Go Further — Garden Tiles

Last time, you found the number of tiles needed to build a walkway around a garden. Work with a partner to analyze your work. What do you notice about relationships between plants and tiles?

Things we discovered: _____

_____

_____

_____

_____

1. Predict how many tiles will be needed for gardens with seven, eight and ten plants.

_____

2. What happens to the number of tiles when you add one more plant?

_____

3. If you had 37 plants, how many tiles would you need? Explain your reasoning.

_____

_____

_____

_____

_____

4. If you had *n* plants, how many tiles would you need? Give your answer in words and as an algebraic expression.

_____

_____

On today's activity: (Circle one) — I need to know more. — I got it.

Date

Today's Challenge ✏ Find strings of digits that can be used to make subtraction expressions with values that are greater than 0.16 but less than 0.26. All of the numbers in the expressions must be less than one. You must supply the zeroes in the ones places and the decimal points. Write each expression and its value.

8	6	6	5
7	4	2	4
5	3	1	3
3	9	7	7

_____

_____

_____

_____

Go Further ✏ **Create your own Math Jumble.** Include at least five subtraction expressions with values that are greater than 0.16 but less than 0.26. All of the numbers in the expressions must be less than one. Have a friend find these expressions in your Math Jumble. Your friend must supply the zeroes in the ones place and the decimal points. Have your friend write each expression and its value. If you disagree on the expressions or their values, go back and check your work. Edit if necessary.

_____

_____

_____

_____

_____

Friend's name _____

On today's activity: (Circle one) ✏ I need to know more. ✏ I got it.

Name _____ **Date** _____ **69**

Get Started Fill in the grid with the correct answer. Use the rules for divisibility to find the number that is divisible by six but not by four.

(A) 2350 _____

(B) 1326 _____

(C) 3112 _____

(D) 3528 _____

Today's Challenge Fill in appropriate grid with the correct answer. Use divisibility rules to help you explain your reasoning.

1. Which of these numbers is divisible by nine and by five?

   (A) 1020 _____

   (B) 2016 _____

   (C) 1440 _____

   (D) 1650 _____

2. Which of these numbers is not divisible by 15?

   (A) 1080 _____

   (B) 800 _____

   (C) 1890 _____

   (D) 1995 _____

3. What advice would you give to someone taking a test involving divisibility testing? Think especially about numbers for which you don't have a rule (for example, 12, 15, or 24).

   _____

   _____

   _____

   _____

   _____

   _____

On today's activity: (Circle one) I need to know more. I got it.

Name

Date

Today's Challenge Fill in the table by rounding the given number.

	Round to the Nearest Tenth	Number	Round to the Nearest Hundredth
1.		0.462	
2.		1.013	
3.		0.892	
4.		0.612	
5.		0.445	
6.		9.496	
7.		15.012	
8.		4.312	
9.		0.345	
10.		17.4347	

Go Further

11. Think of at least four numbers that round to 0.8 when rounding to the nearest tenth. Two must be greater than 0.8 and two less than 0.8.

    _____

12. Think of at least four numbers that round to 0.80 when rounding to the nearest hundredth. Two must be greater than 0.80 and two less than 0.80.

    _____

On today's activity: (Circle one) I need to know more. I got it.

Name **Date** **71**

Today's Challenge — Math on a Pool Table

The angle at which a ball hits the side of a pool table is congruent to the angle it bounces off the edge of the table. A ball is hit at a 45° angle from point A on each 'pool table' below. Assume that the ball will travel until it reaches another corner or returns to point A. For the tables below, record the dimensions (horizontal, then vertical) and the first corner the ball hits.

1.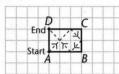

Dimensions _3 × 2_

Start _A_   End _D_

2.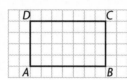

Dimensions _____

Start _A_ End _____

3.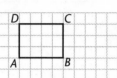

Dimensions _____

Start _A_ End _____

4.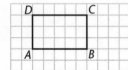

Dimensions _____

Start _A_ End _____

5.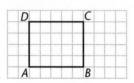

Dimensions _____

Start _A_ End _____

6.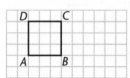

Dimensions _____

Start _A_ End _____

7.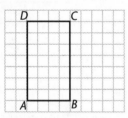

Dimensions _____

Start _A_ End _____

8.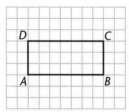

Dimensions _____

Start _A_ End _____

9.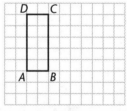

Dimensions _____

Start _A_ End _____

10.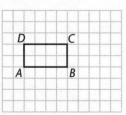

Dimensions _____

Start _A_ End _____

11.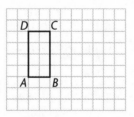

Dimensions _____

Start _A_ End _____

12.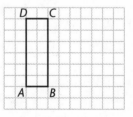

Dimensions _____

Start _A_ End _____

On today's activity: (Circle one) — I need to know more. — I got it.

Name

Date

Go Further — Math on a Pool Table

Work with a partner to check your work on page 72. For the first nine grids, try to discover relationships between the dimensions and where the ball stops.

Things we discovered:

1. List all the grids for which the ball stops at point B. What do you notice about those grids?

_____

_____

2. List all the grids for which the ball stops at point C. What do you notice about those grids?

_____

_____

3. List all the grids for which the ball stops at point D. What do you notice about those grids?

_____

_____

From the answers to the last three questions, you might assume that, for a table with even dimensions, the ball will stop at point A. However, the last three grids contradict that conjecture.

4. Divide both length and width of those rectangles by the greatest common factor. How do the resulting numbers help you predict where the balls will stop?

_____

_____

_____

_____

On today's activity: (Circle one) — I need to know more. — I got it.

Name   Date   **73**

Go Further 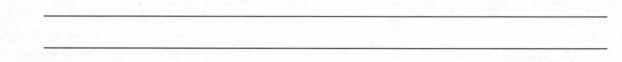 **Follow the directions to mark numbers in the grid.** Some will be marked more than once.

45	108	27	95
54	36	50	90
9	72	65	24
63	48	18	99

1. Cross out all numbers that are multiples of five.

2. Circle all numbers that are less than or equal to the number of ounces in one pound.

3. Star all numbers that are less than the number of minutes in $\frac{3}{4}$ hour.

4. Box all multiples of nine.

5. Which number is not marked? _____

6. Circle all of the numbers in this box that are multiples of nine.

126	145	162	1008	236	420	919	702	4518

7. Explain how you decided which numbers in exercise 6 to circle.

_____

_____

On today's activity: (Circle one) 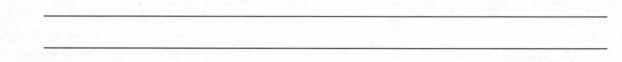 I need to know more. 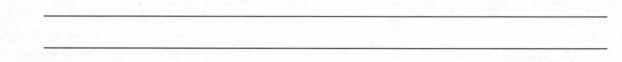 I got it.

Get Started Fill in the circle of the correct answer. Which of the following expressions are equivalent to 44 + 37?

(A) 44 + 40 − 3   (B) 40 + 4 + 40 − 3   (C) 45 − 1 + 40 − 3

Use an equivalent expression to find the sum of 44 and 37. _____

Today's Challenge Fill in the circles by all expressions that are equivalent to the original expression, then compute the sum mentally.

1. 73 + 29
   (A) 70 + 30 + 4
   (B) 72 + 30
   (C) 70 + 20 + 9

   Sum: _____

2. 136 + 58
   (A) 134 + 60
   (B) 136 + 60
   (C) 136 + 60 − 2

   Sum: _____

3. 38 + 56
   (A) 30 + 60 + 8
   (B) 40 + 60 − 6
   (C) 40 + 60 − 4

   Sum: _____

4. 167 + 98
   (A) 170 + 100 − 4
   (B) 167 + 100 − 2
   (C) 165 + 100

   Sum: _____

5. 126 + 47
   (A) 120 + 50 + 13
   (B) 125 + 50 − 3
   (C) 126 + 50 − 3

   Sum: _____

6. 358 + 234
   (A) 360 + 230 + 2
   (B) 350 + 230 + 12
   (C) 350 + 240 + 4

   Sum: _____

7. What advice would you give to a student who was struggling with mental addition?

   _____

   _____

   _____

On today's activity: (Circle one) I need to know more. I got it.

Name

Date

Today's Challenge Fill in the blanks in this chart to show values represented in equivalent forms. Write all fractions in simplest form.

	Fraction	Decimal	Percent
1.			30%
2.		0.75	
3.	$\frac{1}{8}$		
4.			$33\frac{1}{3}\%$
5.		0.4	
6.	$\frac{1}{10}$		
7.			125%
8.	$\frac{3}{5}$		
9.		0.65	
10.			55%

Go Further

11. Write these fractions, decimals, and percents in order from least to greatest.

40%	0.65
$\frac{1}{4}$	
30%	0.05
$\frac{1}{8}$	
85%	0.35
$\frac{9}{10}$	

On today's activity: (Circle one) I need to know more. I got it.

Date

Today's Challenge — Multiplication Stars and Four

There are many interesting patterns which arise when you multiply by certain numbers. Today you will collect data about multiples of four.

1. 0 ×4	**2.** 1 ×4	**3.** 2 ×4	**4.** 3 ×4	**5.** 4 ×4
6. 5 ×4	**7.** 6 ×4	**8.** 7 ×4	**9.** 8 ×4	**10.** 9 ×4
11. 10 ×4	**12.** 11 ×4	**13.** 12 ×4	**14.** 13 ×4	**15.** 14 ×4
16. 15 ×4	**17.** 16 ×4	**18.** 17 ×4	**19.** 18 ×4	**20.** 19 ×4
21. 20 ×4	**22.** 21 ×4	**23.** 22 ×4	**24.** 23 ×4	**25.** 24 ×4
26. 25 ×4	**27.** 26 ×4	**28.** 27 ×4	**29.** 28 ×4	**30.** 29 ×4
31. 60 ×4	**32.** 61 ×4	**33.** 62 ×4	**34.** 63 ×4	**35.** 64 ×4
36. 65 ×4	**37.** 66 ×4	**38.** 67 ×4	**39.** 68 ×4	**40.** 69 ×4

On today's activity: (Circle one) — I need to know more. — I got it.

Name

Date

Go Further ✐ Multiplication Stars and Four

Work with a partner and study the products you found on page 77. Look for patterns in the ones and tens digits in your products. What patterns do you notice?

Things we discovered: _____

_____

_____

_____

_____

1. Write the pattern in the ones digits of multiples of four.

    _____

2. Examine these circles. In the first circle, start at zero and, in order, draw line segments to the ones digits of the products of four and the numbers one through five. In the second circle, connect ones digits of the products of four and the numbers six through ten. In the third circle, connect the ones digits of the products of four and the numbers 56 through 60.

    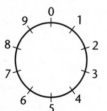 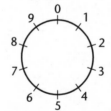 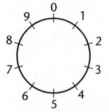

3. Did you need to compute the multiples of four for exercise 2? _____ If yes, edit your rule for patterns in the multiples of four. Write your new rule here.

    _____

4. If you multiply 34 by each of the numbers 21 through 30, does the pattern you discovered still predict the ones digits of your products? Explain.

    _____

    _____

On today's activity: (Circle one) ✐ I need to know more. ▢ I got it.

Date

Get Started

1. Complete the table.

Quadrilateral	Pairs of Parallel Sides	Pairs of Congruent Sides	Pairs of Congruent Angles	Number of Right Angles
Trapezoid				
Parallelogram				
Rectangle				
Rhombus				
Kite				

Go Further

2. Solve this riddle.

   Clues:
   • I have one pair of parallel sides.
   • I have no congruent angles.
   • I have no congruent sides.
   • I have no right angles.

   What is my name? _____

3. Fill in the blanks to make a Quadrilateral Riddle.

   • I have _____ parallel sides.
   • I have _____ congruent angles.
   • I have _____ congruent sides.
   • I have _____ right angles.

   What is my name? _____

4. Now write your own riddle for a friend to solve.

   Clues: _____

   _____

   _____

   What is my name? _____

   Friend's name _____

On today's activity: (Circle one) I need to know more. I got it.

Name

Date

Get Started These expressions have the same value as 63 − 28. Explain how each has been rewritten to make mental subtraction easier. The first is done for you.

A. 65 − 30   _Think of a number line. The distance between 63 and 28 is the difference._

To make the numbers easier to work with yet keep the distance between them the same,

add two to both the 63 and the 28.

B. 63 − 23 − 5 _____

_____

_____

C. 63 − 30 + 2 _____

_____

_____

Which expression do you prefer? _____

What is the value of the expression 63 − 28? _____

Today's Challenge Write an expression that is equivalent to the original expression and then use it to compute the difference mentally. Explain why your equivalent expression works.

1. 74 − 39 _____

2. 132 − 58 _____

3. 234 − 98 _____

4. 136 − 67 _____

5. What advice would you give to a student who wanted to use mental math to improve his or her test results?

_____

_____

_____

_____

On today's activity: (Circle one) I need to know more. I got it.

Today's Challenge — Fill in this table by adding the integer at the top of the column to the integer at the left of the row.

+	−5	−2	1	5
1. −4				
2. −3				
3. 5				

Go Further

4. Write four different integer-addition problems that have a sum of −4.

Example: 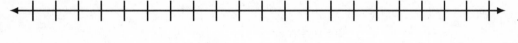 $^-6 + 2 = {}^-4$

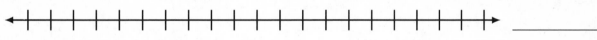 _____

_____

_____

_____

5. Write four different integer-addition problems that have a sum of 2.

 _____

_____

_____

_____

On today's activity: (Circle one) — I need to know more. — I got it.

Name _____ **Date** _____

Today's Challenge — Multiplication Stars and Six

Today you will collect data about multiples of six.

1. 0 ×6	2. 1 ×6	3. 2 ×6	4. 3 ×6	5. 4 ×6
6. 5 ×6	7. 6 ×6	8. 7 ×6	9. 8 ×6	10. 9 ×6
11. 10 ×6	12. 11 ×6	13. 12 ×6	14. 13 ×6	15. 14 ×6
16. 15 ×6	17. 16 ×6	18. 17 ×6	19. 18 ×6	20. 19 ×6
21. 20 ×6	22. 21 ×6	23. 22 ×6	24. 23 ×6	25. 24 ×6
26. 25 ×6	27. 26 ×6	28. 27 ×6	29. 28 ×6	30. 29 ×6
31. 60 ×6	32. 61 ×6	33. 62 ×6	34. 63 ×6	35. 64 ×6
36. 65 ×6	37. 66 ×6	38. 67 ×6	39. 68 ×6	40. 69 ×6

On today's activity: (Circle one) — I need to know more. — I got it.

Name

Date

Go Further — **Multiplication Stars and Six**

Work with a partner to study the products you found on page 82. Look for patterns in the ones and tens digits in your products. Write your discoveries here.

Things we discovered: _____

_____

_____

_____

_____

1. Write the pattern in the ones digits of multiples of six.

   _____

2. Examine these circles. In the first circle, start at zero. In order, draw line segments to the ones digits of the products of six and the numbers one through five. In the second circle, connect ones digits of the products of six and the numbers six through ten. In the third circle, connect the ones digits of the products of six and the numbers 56 through 60.

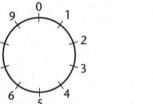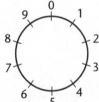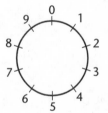

3. Did you, need to compute the multiples of six for exercise 2? _____
   If yes, edit your rule for patterns in the multiples of six. Write your new rule here.

   _____

4. If you multiply 56 by each of the numbers 41 through 50, does the pattern you discovered still predict the ones digits of your products? Explain.

   _____

   _____

On today's activity: (Circle one) — I need to know more. — I got it.

Name

Date

Today's Challenge   **Fill in the table.** Be sure to mark parallel segments, congruent parts, and right angles.

	Name	Sketch		Name	Sketch
1.	Isosceles Triangle		2.	_____	
3.	_____		4.	Parallelogram	
5.	_____		6.	Obtuse Triangle	
7.	Hexagon		8.	_____	
9.	Circle		10.	_____	

On today's activity: (Circle one)   I need to know more.   I got it.

Get Started Mark the letter of each correctly solved problem.

Here are four examples of Mandy's work on a test on area. Mark the letter of each exercise that Mandy has correctly solved. Then correct her mistakes.

A. 32 square feet

B. 18 square feet

C. 60 square centimeters

Today's Challenge Mark the letter of the correct answer.

1. For which of these figures do you think Mandy would find the correct area? Explain why or why not. Provide the correct area for each figure.

A. _____ Area: _____

B. _____ Area: _____

On a separate piece of paper, draw and label a rectangle with the same area as each parallelogram.

2. Area: _____

3. Area: _____

4. Area: _____

5. Area: _____

6. What advice would you give Mandy about finding the areas of parallelograms and rectangles?

_____

_____

_____

_____

_____

_____

On today's activity: (Circle one) I need to know more. I got it.

Name **Date**

Today's Challenge Fill in the missing number to make the two measurements equivalent. The first is done for you.

	Amount	Measurement Equivalent
1.	Two weeks	<u>14</u> days
2.	Three feet	_____ inches
3.	One dollar	_____ nickels
4.	$\frac{3}{4}$ of a minute	_____ seconds
5.	One pound	_____ ounces
6.	Two gallons	_____ quarts
7.	One yard	_____ inches
8.	$\frac{1}{2}$ of a day	_____ hours
9.	Three dollars	_____ quarters
10.	One kilometer	_____ meters
11.	$\frac{1}{10}$ of an hour	_____ minutes

Go Further Fill in the table.

12. Is this fraction of an hour equivalent to a whole number of minutes? (For example, $\frac{1}{7}$ of an hour is not a whole number of minutes but $\frac{1}{6}$ of a hour is.) Write yes or no.

$\frac{1}{2}$	
$\frac{1}{3}$	
$\frac{1}{10}$	
$\frac{1}{5}$	
$\frac{1}{4}$	
$\frac{1}{8}$	
$\frac{1}{9}$	
$\frac{1}{12}$	

On today's activity: (Circle one) I need to know more. I got it.

Date

Today's Challenge   The Staircase Challenge

Use colored squares or graph paper to form staircases that follow the pattern shown in the diagram. Count the number of squares used for each one. Fill in the table by recording the number of squares needed to make each staircase.

Staircase Number (*n*)	1	2	3	4	5	6	7	8	9	10
Number of Squares										

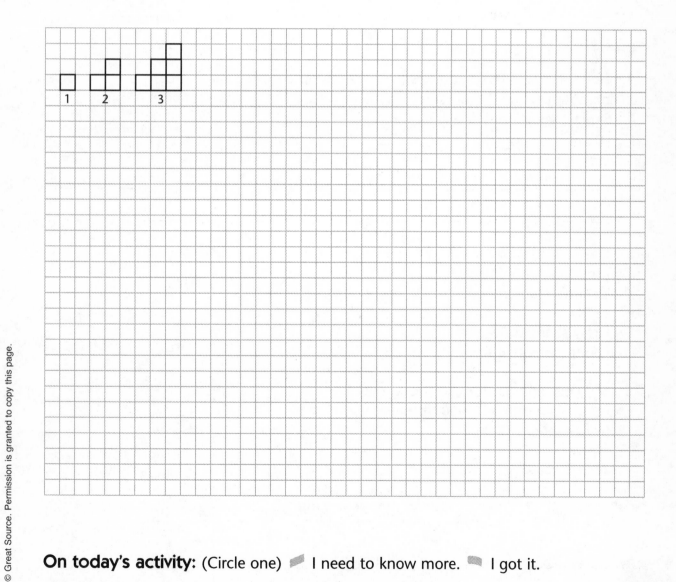

On today's activity: (Circle one)   I need to know more.   I got it.

Name   Date

Go Further ⬥ The Staircase Challenge

Review the work you did on page 87. Work with a partner. Study the table to find patterns in the number of squares needed to make each new staircase.

Things we discovered: _____

_____

_____

_____

_____

1. Find a formula that expresses the relationship between the staircase number (n) and the number of squares needed to build the staircase (s). Explain your formula.

   _____

   _____

   _____

2. Use your formula to predict the number of squares in staircase 15. _____

3. Draw staircase 15 and count the squares. _____

4. Did your answers for exercises 2 and 3 match? If not, revise your formula from exercise 1.

   _____

5. Predict the number of squares in staircase 20. _____

On today's activity: (Circle one) ⬥ I need to know more. ⬥ I got it.

Name

Date

Today's Challenge Look for strings of digits that can be used to write multiplication equations with products greater than 300 but less than 350. Each equation must include a one-digit and a two-digit factor. The product *will* be included as part of the string.

5	5	1	3
8	4	6	3
1	5	3	2
3	6	0	5

_____

_____

_____

_____

Go Further **Create your own Math Jumble.** Include at least three pairs of numbers with a product greater than 300 and less than 350. Each equation must include a one-digit and a two-digit factor. Remember to *include* the product in each string you make. Have a friend find these equations in your Math Jumble. If you disagree on the equations, check your work. Edit if necessary.

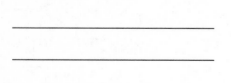

_____

_____

_____

Friend's name _____

On today's activity: (Circle one) I need to know more. I got it.

Name **Date** **89**

Get Started Work with a partner to explain the steps in this problem.

Problem: Find the surface area of this cube.

Solution:

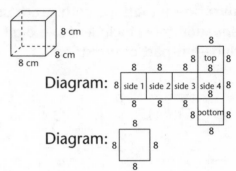

Draw and label a net of the cube so you can see the shapes and measures of the surfaces.

Diagram: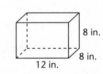

Look at each face of the cube and find any that are the same.

Diagram:

There are six identical squares.

Find the area of one of the identical squares.

$8 \times 8 = 64$

Find the area of six identical squares.

$64 \times 6 = 384$

Write a clear, complete answer to the problem.

The surface area of the cube is 384 square centimeters.

Today's Challenge

1. On another sheet of paper, write a constructed response.
   Problem: Find the surface area of this rectangular prism.
   Solution:

2. What advice would you give to someone trying to calculate the surface area of a triangular prism?

On today's activity: (Circle one) I need to know more. I got it.

90 **Name**

Date

Today's Challenge ✏ Fill in the table by finding the mean, median, or mode as indicated.

	Numerical Data	Find the . . .
1.	5, 5, and 10	Median
2.	5, 10, and 5	Mode
3.	5, 10, 5, and 20	Mean
4.	12, 15, and 21	Mean
5.	21, 12, 15, and 21	Median
6.	21, 12, 24, and 15	Mode
7.	20, 24, and 31	Mean
8.	1, 40, and 4	Median
9.	1, 4, and 40	Mean
10.	6.5, 1.25, and 7.4	Mean
11.	25, 75, 24, and 11	Median

Go Further ✏ Fill in the table.

12.	10, 15, and 20	Mean		Median
13.	10, 15, and 200	Mean		Median

14. Look back at the data for exercises 12 and 13. If a data set contains a number that is very different from the rest of the data, will that number affect the mean or median more? Explain.

_____

15. When will the median be one of the numbers in a set of data? When will the median *not* be one of the numbers in the set of data?

_____

On today's activity: (Circle one) ✏ I need to know more. ✏ I got it.

Name _____   **Date** _____

Today's Challenge ✏ Use Patterns to Add Numbers

When Carl Gauss was eight years old in 1785, he added the numbers 1–100 in his head in only a few seconds! It is impossible to know how the young Gauss accomplished this, but it is certain that he observed some patterns to the numbers that enabled him to add them so quickly.

Use patterns you notice in the hundred chart to find a quick way to find the sum of the numbers 1–100 without just adding them in order.

1	2	3	4	5	6	7	8	9	10
11	12	13	14	15	16	17	18	19	20
21	22	23	24	25	26	27	28	29	30
31	32	33	34	35	36	37	38	39	40
41	42	43	44	45	46	47	48	49	50
51	52	53	54	55	56	57	58	59	60
61	62	63	64	65	66	67	68	69	70
71	72	73	74	75	76	77	78	79	80
81	82	83	84	85	86	87	88	89	90
91	92	93	94	95	96	97	98	99	100

1	2	3	4	5	6	7	8	9	10
11	12	13	14	15	16	17	18	19	20
21	22	23	24	25	26	27	28	29	30
31	32	33	34	35	36	37	38	39	40
41	42	43	44	45	46	47	48	49	50
51	52	53	54	55	56	57	58	59	60
61	62	63	64	65	66	67	68	69	70
71	72	73	74	75	76	77	78	79	80
81	82	83	84	85	86	87	88	89	90
91	92	93	94	95	96	97	98	99	100

On today's activity: (Circle one) ✏ I need to know more. ✏ I got it.

Name Date

Go Further — Use Patterns to Add Numbers

Last time, you probably found a way to compute the sum of the numbers 1–100 that was faster than adding the numbers in order. Is your method faster than using a calculator to add all the numbers 1–200 in order? What about methods others in your class invented? Try a few methods with and without a calculator and write what you learned.

Things we discovered: _____

_____

_____

_____

_____

_____

_____

_____

_____

In mathematics there are usually many ways to solve a problem. Use what you have learned about adding consecutive numbers.

1. Explain how you would use a calculator to find the sum of 1–400, then find the sum.

   _____

   _____

   _____

   _____

On today's activity: (Circle one) — I need to know more. — I got it.

Name _____ **Date** _____ 93

Go Further Follow the directions to mark polygons in the grid. Some will be marked more than once.

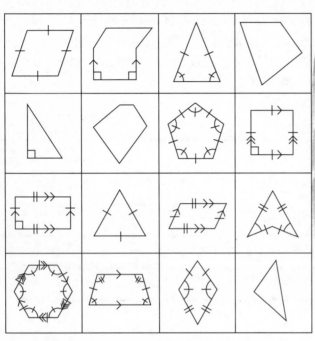

1. Cross out all polygons with more than one right angle.

2. Circle all polygons with no line of symmetry.

3. Star all polygons with no parallel sides.

4. Box all polygons with an odd number of sides.

5. Shade all squares containing polygons with at least two lines of symmetry.

6. Check all polygons with no congruent angles.

7. Which polygon is not crossed out? _____

8. Write at least three statements that describe that polygon.

_____

_____

_____

On today's activity: (Circle one) I need to know more. I got it.

Get Started Fill in the circle of the correct answer.
Which expression is equivalent to 29 × 18?

(A) 30 × 20 − 3   (B) 30 × 18 − 30   (C) 30 × 18 − 18

Explain why the expression you chose is equivalent to 29 × 18.

_____

Use your expression to find the value of 29 × 18. _____

Today's Challenge Fill in the circle of the expression that is equivalent to the
original expression. Use mental multiplication to find the product.

1. 29 × 23   2. 22 × 14

  (A) 20 × 20 + 9 × 3   (A) 20 × 14 + 2 × 14

  (B) 30 × 23 − 23   (B) 20 × 16

  (C) 30 × 22   (C) 20 × 10 + 2 × 4

  Product: _____   Product: _____

3. What property transforms 38 × 24 to (40 × 24) − (2 × 24)?

  (A) Distributive Property

  (B) Associative Property of Multiplication

  (C) Identity Element for Multiplication

4. Show how the property you chose for exercise 3 transforms 38 × 24 to
   (40 × 24) − (2 × 24), then evaluate the expression.

   _____

   _____

   _____

5. What advice would you give to a student who is trying to increase speed and
   accuracy on multiplication tests where calculators are not available?

   _____

   _____

On today's activity: (Circle one) I need to know more. I got it.

Name   Date

Today's Challenge Fill in the rest of this table by multiplying *Number* by 0.01, 0.1, 10 and 100.

	Multiply by 0.01	Multiply by 0.1	Number	Multiply by 10	Multiply by 100
1.			780		
2.			1.013		
3.			80.3		
4.			1670		
5.			4.05		
6.			150		
7.			1.602		
8.			431.2		
9.			3.45		
10.			28,432		

Go Further Given one factor and the product, find the second factor in the multiplication expression.

	First Factor	Second Factor	Product
11.	2770		277
12.	95.06		0.9506
13.	0.915		91.5
14.	89.12		891.2
15.	942		94.2

On today's activity: (Circle one) I need to know more. I got it.

Name

Date

Today's Challenge — **Making Picture Frames**

Make diagrams and record your data for these problems.

You have four frame pieces that are all the same length. They are all an inch wide.

1 in.
— 5 in. —

You have to make a frame like this for a picture.

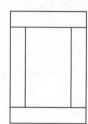

Draw diagrams.

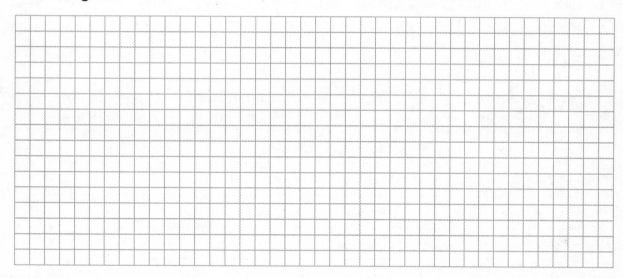

	Length of Pieces	Width	Dimensions of Picture	Area of Picture
1.	5 inches	1 inch		
2.	6 inches	1 inch		
3.	7 inches	1 inch		
4.	8 inches	1 inch		
5.	9 inches	1 inch		
6.	10 inches	1 inch		

On today's activity: (Circle one) — I need to know more. — I got it.

Name

Date

Go Further — Making Picture Frames

Work with a partner to check and analyze your work on page 97. Look for a pattern to help you predict the dimensions of pictures in similar frames.

Things we discovered: _____

_____

A useful mathematical pattern is one you can change to solve another problem.

1. Write an equation to describe the relationship between the length of a frame piece (ℓ) and the area of the framed picture on page 97. _____

2. Fill in the table.

Length of Pieces	Width	Dimensions of Picture	Area of Picture
5 inches	2 inches		
6 inches	2 inches		
7 inches	2 inches		
8 inches	2 inches		
9 inches	2 inches		
10 inches	2 inches		

3. How did you change your equation to fit the new problems? _____

4. Suppose the frame pieces were three inches wide and all the same length. What equation would you use to compute the dimensions of a framed picture?

_____

5. Which frame pieces in the table for exercise 2 would not work if they were three inches wide? _____

_____

On today's activity: (Circle one) — I need to know more. — I got it.

Date

Get Started ✏ **For each question, write *yes* or *no*.** Remember to calculate the change with the fewest coins and bills.

I bought an item for $2.65. I paid with a ten-dollar bill.

1. Does my change include any pennies? _____

2. Does my change include more than one dime? _____

3. Does my change include more than one quarter? _____

4. Is my change more than $7.25? _____

I bought an item for $3.16. I paid with a ten-dollar bill.

5. Does my change include any nickels? _____

6. Does my change include more than two pennies? _____

7. Does my change include more than one dime? _____

8. Is my change less than $8.90? _____

Go Further

9. Solve this riddle.

    Clues: • I bought an item for $3.68.

    • I paid with a ten-dollar bill.

    • I received change using the fewest coins and bills.

    What coins and bills do I have? _____

10. Write your own riddle for a friend to solve.

    Clues: _____

    _____

    _____

    What coins and bills do I have? _____

    Friend's name _____

On today's activity: (Circle one) ◢ I need to know more. ◣ I got it.

Name _____ **Date** _____ **99**

Get Started Circle the letters by the correct answers.

Here are four examples of Titus' answers to a test on solving proportions. Fill in the second grid with the correct solution to each proportion.

(A) $\frac{2}{4} = \frac{n}{12}$ (B) $\frac{3}{8} = \frac{n}{40}$ (C) $\frac{4}{7} = \frac{n}{49}$ (D) $\frac{1}{6} = \frac{n}{24}$

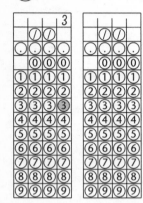 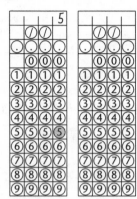 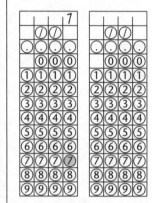

Today's Challenge Fill in the appropriate grid with the correct answer.

1. $\frac{n}{24} = \frac{5}{6}$ 2. $\frac{2}{3} = \frac{n}{18}$ 3. $\frac{4}{7} = \frac{n}{63}$ 4. $\frac{n}{30} = \frac{5}{6}$

5. $\frac{4}{9} = \frac{n}{54}$ 6. $\frac{3}{4} = \frac{n}{48}$ 7. $\frac{n}{15} = \frac{3}{5}$ 8. $\frac{n}{20} = \frac{3}{5}$

1.   2.   3.   4.   5.   6.   7.   8.

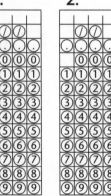   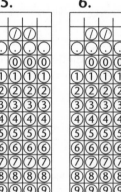 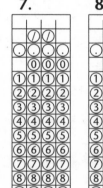 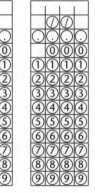

9. What advice would you give Titus about solving proportions?

_____

_____

_____

On today's activity: (Circle one) I need to know more. I got it.

100 **Name**

Date

Today's Challenge

1. Draw two different five-sided polygons.

2. Draw two different eight-sided polygons.

3. Draw two different quadrilaterals with four congruent sides. One should have congruent angles, the other should not.

4. Draw two different polygons with six sides.

5. Draw a three-sided polygon with congruent sides.

6. Draw a four-sided figure. It must have two sets of congruent sides but *no* parallel sides.

7. Draw the angle that measures exactly 90°.

8. Draw two different acute angles.

9. Draw a cylinder.

10. Draw a cube.

Go Further

11. Label the figures you drew for exercises 1–7 with their names.

12. How are the sketches for exercises 9 and 10 different from those for exercises 1–6?

_____

_____

On today's activity: (Circle one)   I need to know more.   I got it.

Name _____   **Date** _____

Today's Challenge — Follow the Bouncing Ball Challenge

A special ball is dropped from a height of one yard. It always bounces back to one half the height it started from. Assume that the distance traveled for a bounce is measured from the floor and back to the floor. Draw a diagram and finish filling in the table.

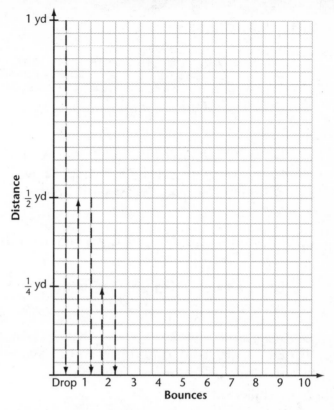

Bounce	Up (in yards)	Down (in yards)	Distance (in yards)	Running Total (in yards)
Drop		1	1	1
1	$\frac{1}{2}$	$\frac{1}{2}$	1	2
2				
3				
4				
5				
6				
7				
8				
9				
10				

On today's activity: (Circle one) — I need to know more. — I got it.

Date

Go Further ⬤ Follow the Bouncing Ball Challenge

Work with a partner. Study and check your work on page 102. Look for patterns and interesting facts about how far the ball travels.

Things we discovered: _____

_____

_____

You can often use what you learned from a problem to solve a related one.

1. Explain how making a careful diagram helped solve the bouncing ball problem.

   _____

   _____

   _____

2. Will the distance traveled ever be as much as three feet? Explain.

   _____

   _____

3. Use what you know about making a list and using a pattern to solve this problem about another bouncing ball. This ball bounces one-third of the way back up after bouncing. How far has this ball traveled when it hits the floor the fifth time after being dropped from a height of one foot?

   _____

Diagram

On today's activity: (Circle one) ⬤ I need to know more. ⬤ I got it.

Name **Date**

Today's Challenge Shade the correct percent, or name the percent shaded.

1. 40%

2. _____

3. 10%

4. _____

5. _____

6. 75%

7. 60%

8. _____

9. 5%

10. _____

On today's activity: (Circle one) I need to know more. I got it.

Date

Get Started — Mark the letter of the correct response.

Which of the shaded squares does *not* represent 20% of the whole square?

A.   **B.**   **C.**   **D.**

Today's Challenge — Mark the letter of the correct response.

1. Which of the shaded squares does *not* represent 75% of the whole square?

   A.   **B.**   **C.**   **D.**

2. Which of the shaded squares does *not* represent 18% of the whole square?

   A.   **B.**   **C.**   **D.**

3. Which of the shaded squares does *not* represent 7% of the whole square?

   A.   **B.**   **C.**   **D.**

4. If you were taking a test and needed to draw a diagram to show 25%, which should you use and why?

   A. This diagram is most creative.

   C. This diagram is easy to read as 25%.

   B. This diagram is most accurate.

   D. This diagram is easy to draw.

5. What advice would you give to students reading or drawing percent diagrams on tests?

   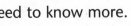

   _____

On today's activity: (Circle one) — I need to know more. — I got it.

Name   Date   105

Today's Challenge Use mental math to fill in the table. Find the given percent of each number.

		10%	25%	$33\frac{1}{3}$%	50%
1.	120				
2.	300				
3.	4800				
4.	6000				
5.	360				

Go Further

6. Look at the table. Which column will help you find 5% of each number?

_____

7. Find 5% of the numbers in exercises 1–5.

_____

8. Use the work you've already done in exercise 7 to help you find 15% of each number in exercises 1–5.

_____

9. What did you do to solve exercise 8? _____

_____

10. Use the work you've already done to find $66\frac{2}{3}$% of the numbers in exercises 1–5.

_____

11. Explain what you did to solve exercise 10. _____

_____

On today's activity: (Circle one) I need to know more. I got it.

Date

Today's Challenge — Minimum Perimeter

You may use the colored squares to form rectangles with side-lengths that are whole numbers. Fill in the table.

1. For each area given, record all possible rectangles and their perimeters. The first is started for you.

Area of Rectangle (in square feet)	Dimensions of Rectangle (in feet)	Perimeter of Rectangle (in feet)
12	1 × 12	26
24		
36		
48		

2. On another sheet of paper, explain any strategies you used for finding all possible rectangles with a given area.

On today's activity: (Circle one) — I need to know more. — I got it.

Name   Date   107

Go Further — Minimum Perimeter

Work with a partner. Study your work on page 107 and look for a quick way to tell which rectangle with a given area will have the shortest perimeter. Write your discoveries here.

Things we discovered: _____

_____

_____

Many times the findings in a few problems can be used to apply to all problems like them.

1. Find all of the base/height combinations for these triangles. Use only whole-number dimensions.

Area (in square feet)	Base (in feet)	Height (in feet)
12		
9		

Area (in square feet)	Base (in feet)	Height (in feet)
6		
3		

2. How did you use the **Things we discovered** to complete exercise 1?

_____

_____

On today's activity: (Circle one) — I need to know more. — I got it.

Date

Today's Challenge Find strings of digits that can be used to write addition expressions with values that are greater than 1.75 but less than 2.25. You must supply placeholders and decimal points. Write each expression and its value.

5	6	4	8
6	3	1	2
4	5	3	7
7	1	6	5

_____

_____

_____

_____

_____

Go Further Create your own Math Jumble. Include at least five addition expressions with values that are greater than 1.75 but less than 2.25. Have a friend find these expressions in your Math Jumble. Your friend must supply placeholders and decimal points. Have your friend write each expression and its value. If you disagree on expressions or their values, check your work. Edit if necessary.

_____

_____

_____

_____

Friend's name _____

On today's activity: (Circle one) I need to know more. I got it.

Name   Date

Get Started Mark the letter of the correct answer.

Lois Terms was taking a test. Here are four examples of Lois's work. Mark the letter of each proportion that Lois has solved correctly, then correct her mistakes.

A. Scale: $\frac{3 \text{ inches}}{4 \text{ feet}} = \frac{n}{8 \text{ feet}}$ ___n = 6 feet_____

B. Freeway survey: $\frac{6 \text{ cars}}{6 \text{ people}} = \frac{n \text{ cars}}{18 \text{ people}}$ ___n = 18_____

C. Nuts picked from tree: $\frac{5 \text{ cups}}{5 \text{ pounds}} = \frac{n}{8 \text{ pounds}}$ ___n = 8 pounds_____

D. Calendar planning: $\frac{16 \text{ weeks}}{n \text{ months}} = \frac{4 \text{ weeks}}{1 \text{ month}}$ ___n = 4_____

Today's Challenge

1. Which of these proportions do you think Lois would solve correctly? Explain your thinking about each answer choice.

   A. $\frac{3 \text{ feet}}{1 \text{ yard}} = \frac{9 \text{ feet}}{x}$ _____

   B. $\frac{100 \text{ centimeters}}{10 \text{ decimeters}} = \frac{1000 \text{ centimeters}}{x \text{ decimeters}}$ _____

For exercises 2–11, fill in the box or blank.

2. $\frac{3 \text{ times}}{4 \text{ years}} = \frac{\boxed{}}{24 \text{ years}}$

3. $\frac{\boxed{}}{16 \text{ days}} = \frac{3 \text{ tests}}{8 \text{ days}}$

4. A package of eight mixed onions has a ratio of two red to six yellow onions. You have 144 red onions. If you have _____ yellow onions, you can make _____ packages of mixed onions with none left over.

5. A recipe calls for three cups of dry noodles and two cups of broth. You only have _____ of dry noodles, so you can use only one cup of broth.

6. To make a light green paint, you use 15 drops of blue for every pint of yellow. If you start with a quart of yellow, you must add _____ drops of blue.

7. What advice would you give Lois about solving proportions?

   _____

   _____

   _____

   _____

Today's Challenge Use the answer to one exercise as your starting point for the next exercise. If you fill in all the answers correctly, you should end up with what you started with.

		Answer
1.	Start with $20.00. What is five times this much?	
2.	I spent 60% of this amount of money. How much did I have left?	
3.	How many $8.00 books can I buy with this amount?	
4.	I have saved my $3.50 allowance for this many weeks. How much do I have now?	
5.	I spend a ten-dollar bill, a quarter, and a dime. How much do I have left?	
6.	I made this amount from three bills and two coins. What is the value of the coin that is worth the least?	
7.	If I have a collection of 140 coins that are each worth this much, how much is my collection worth?	
8.	If a magazine costs $3.50 how many can I buy with the nickels in my collection?	
9.	I want to buy this many boxes of popcorn at $3.75 each and a soda for $2.25. How much do I need?	
10.	Add a ten-dollar bill and one quarter. How much do I have now?	$20.00

Go Further

11. Using <u>exactly 16 coins</u> per row, make each row worth <u>$1.00</u>. If a block is shaded, you cannot use any of those coins. If a block is open, you must use at least one of those coins.

50¢ half-dollar	25¢ quarter	10¢ dime	5¢ nickel	1¢ penny
▓		▓		
▓	▓			
▓		▓		
▓				
	▓			

On today's activity: (Circle one) I need to know more. I got it.

Name **Date** 111

Today's Challenge — What Is the Message?

You can use what you know about numbers and our number system to find the numbers behind a message.

This message was sent from a son at college to his father, a mathematician. The son hoped the father would appreciate the message because it was part of a math challenge. Each letter stands for a different digit.

1. What digits (0–9) does each letter represent? Keep track of how you solved for each letter. Each letter represents the same digit every time it is used.

_____

_____

_____

_____

2. Since the mathematician did not want to take up too much of his son's time, his reply was a problem with three different possible solutions. Try to find all three. Keep track of how you solved for each letter.

Solution 1	Solution 2	Solution 3

On today's activity: (Circle one) — I need to know more. — I got it.

Date

Go Further — **What is the Message?**

Last time, you should have used some relationships between numbers and addition in our base-ten number system. Work with a friend to check and analyze your work on page 112. Write your discoveries here.

Things we discovered: _____

_____

_____

_____

1. What is the greatest sum for two different one-digit numbers? Explain.

_____

_____

_____

_____

2. You have two different addends. When you need to regroup, what digit is always regrouped into the next column? Explain.

_____

_____

_____

_____

3. Use your discoveries to make up three message sums. Share them with your partner, then edit if necessary.

+	+	+

On today's activity: (Circle one) — I need to know more. — I got it.

Name **Date**

Go Further 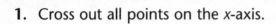 **Follow the directions to mark points in the plane.** Some will be marked more than once.

1. Cross out all points on the *x*-axis.

2. Star all points with *x* = *y*.

3. Circle all points with *x* > *y*.

4. Box all points with *y* = 6.

5. Underline all points with *y* − *x* = 2.

6. Which point is not marked? _____

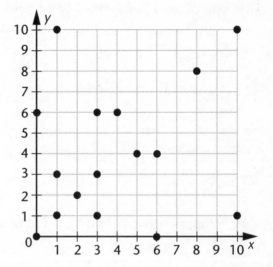

7. Mark each point on this grid that follows these rules.

   • *x* + *y* = 6

   • *x* and *y* are whole numbers

8. Connect your points for exercise 7. What geometric figure have you drawn?

   _____

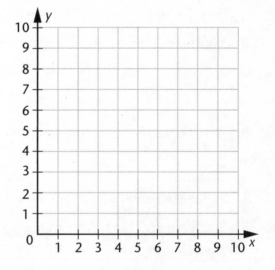

On today's activity: (Circle one) I need to know more. I got it.

114 Name

Date

Get Started 🖋 **Rule out two answer choices.** Explain why you eliminated each, then fill in the circle of the correct answer. Find the approximate area of this triangle. Measurements are rounded.

10 cm / 8 cm / 24 cm / 29 cm

(A) about 232 square centimeters _____

(B) about 116 square centimeters _____

(C) about 96 square centimeters _____

Did you need to use your calculator to choose the answer? Explain.

_____

Today's Challenge 🖋 **Fill in the circle of the correct answer.** Explain now you eliminated wrong choices.

1. Find the area of this triangle.

(A) 440 square feet _____

(B) 440 yards _____

(C) 440 square yards _____

44 yd / 20 yd / 25 yd

Did you need to use your calculator to choose the answer? _____ Explain.

_____

2. Find the area of this figure.

(A) 1.2 square centimeters _____

(B) 0.6 square centimeters _____

(C) 0.12 square centimeters _____

1 cm / 1 cm / 0.6 cm

Did you need to use your calculator to choose the answer? _____ Explain.

_____

3. What advice would you give to a student studying for a test on area of triangles?

_____

_____

_____

_____

_____

_____

On today's activity: (Circle one) 🖋 I need to know more. 🖋 I got it.

Name _____ **Date** _____ 115

Today's Challenge Fill in this table by subtracting the number at the left of the row from the number at the top of the column. Write your difference in simplest form.

−	1	$1\frac{1}{2}$	$1\frac{3}{4}$	$1\frac{5}{6}$
1. $\frac{1}{4}$				
2. $\frac{2}{3}$				
3. $\frac{5}{6}$				

Go Further

4. Write the differences in the table in order from least to greatest.

_____

_____

5. Make your own fraction-addition table for a friend to solve. Write your answers on another piece of paper.

Friend's name

_____

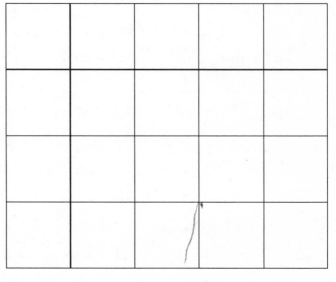

On today's activity: (Circle one) I need to know more. I got it.

Today's Challenge Sifting out Composite Numbers

1. Use this method of crossing out composite numbers in the hundred chart.

   • Cross out one.

   • Circle two and cross out multiples of two.

   • Circle the next unmarked number after two and then cross out all of the multiples of that number.

   • Repeat, circling numbers, and crossing out their multiples until you have checked all numbers in the chart.

1	2	3	4	5	6	7	8	9	10
11	12	13	14	15	16	17	18	19	20
21	22	23	24	25	26	27	28	29	30
31	32	33	34	35	36	37	38	39	40
41	42	43	44	45	46	47	48	49	50
51	52	53	54	55	56	57	58	59	60
61	62	63	64	65	66	67	68	69	70
71	72	73	74	75	76	77	78	79	80
81	82	83	84	85	86	87	88	89	90
91	92	93	94	95	96	97	98	99	100

2. What is special about the circled numbers on your chart?

_____

On today's activity: (Circle one) I need to know more. I got it.

Name Date

Go Further — Sifting out Composite Numbers

Work with a partner to check your work on page 117. Look for patterns in the cross-outs. Write your discoveries here or on another piece of paper.

Things we discovered: _____

_____

_____

_____

You used a method for finding prime numbers that is over two thousand years old. In mathematics, methods many years old can still be used to solve problems today.

1. What patterns in the cross-outs might be used to find primes from 101 to 200?

   _____

   _____

2. Use your patterns to find the primes from 101 to 200.

3. How many primes are between 100 and 200?

   _____

4. Why do you think there are fewer primes between 100 and 200 than between 0 and 100?

   _____

   _____

101	102	103	104	105	106	107	108	109	110
111	112	113	114	115	116	117	118	119	120
121	122	123	124	125	126	127	128	129	130
131	132	133	134	135	136	137	138	139	140
141	142	143	144	145	146	147	148	149	150
151	152	153	154	155	156	157	158	159	160
161	162	163	164	165	166	167	168	169	170
171	172	173	174	175	176	177	178	179	180
181	182	183	184	185	186	187	188	189	190
191	192	193	194	195	196	197	198	199	200

5. What can you say about the number of primes between 200 and 300?

   _____

   _____

On today's activity: (Circle one) — I need to know more. — I got it.

Date

Get Started

1. Label the number line with simplified fractions.

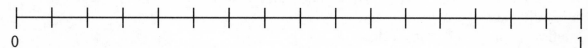

0   1

Go Further   Name a fraction from your number line that answers each riddle.

2. I am greater than $\frac{1}{4}$ but less than $\frac{1}{2}$ and my numerator is three.

   Who am I? _____

3. I am greater than $\frac{1}{2}$ and my numerator is seven.

   Who am I? _____

4. I am between 0 and $\frac{1}{4}$ and the sum of numerator and denominator is 17.

   Who am I? _____

5. Fill in the blanks with fractions to make a measurement riddle.

   Clues: • I am greater than _____

   • I am less than _____.

   • My numerator is _____.

      Who am I? _____

6. Now write your own riddle for a friend to solve.

   Clues: _____

   _____

   _____

   _____

   Who am I? _____

   Friend's name _____

On today's activity: (Circle one)   I need to know more.   I got it.

ABCD Ace the Test

Get Started Study the constructed response.

Problem: Harold Square bought a CD that was on sale. The regular price of the CD was $14.99, but it was on sale at 20% off. Tax in Harold's town is 6%. How much did Harold pay for the CD?

Solution: First, find the sale price.

A.	20% off of 100% is 80%. Find 80% of $14.99.	$14.99 \times 0.8 = 11.992$
B.	11.992 has too many decimal places for money.	Round to $11.99
	Next, add the tax.	
C.	Find the tax: 6% of 11.99	$11.99 \times 0.06 = 0.7194$
D.	0.7194 has too many decimal places.	Round to 0.72.
E.	Add the tax to the price.	$11.99 + 0.72 = 12.71$
F.	Finally, write the answer to the original question.	Harold paid $12.71 for the CD.

Today's Challenge Write constructed responses on a separate sheet of paper.

1. **Problem:** If Harold's parents pay their fuel oil bill within one week, they can save 12%. This month the fuel cost is $196.00. They had a $24.00 credit from last month's bill. How much will Harold's parents save by paying this month's bill within one week?

2. **Problem:** Harold bought two shirts that were on sale. The sale was set up so that if you buy two shirts, then you save 25% of the total cost of the two shirts. The two shirts were priced at $16.99 and $25.99 before the sale. There is no tax on clothing in Harold's state. What did Harold pay for the shirts?

3. What advice would you give to a student preparing for a constructed response test?

_____

_____

_____

_____

_____

_____

On today's activity: (Circle one) I need to know more. I got it.

120 Name

Date

Today's Challenge Which is greater? By how much?

		Which is Greater	How Much Greater
1.	Which is greater, $\frac{1}{3}$ of 21 or $\frac{1}{4}$ of 48?		
2.	Which is greater, $\frac{1}{7}$ of 35 or $\frac{1}{9}$ of 36?		
3.	Which is greater, $\frac{1}{6}$ of 102 or $\frac{1}{2}$ of 36?		
4.	Which is greater, $\frac{3}{8}$ of 48 or $\frac{5}{9}$ of 27?		
5.	Which is greater, $\frac{2}{3}$ of 30 or $\frac{3}{8}$ of 56?		
6.	Which is greater, $\frac{5}{8}$ of 96 or $\frac{7}{8}$ of 72?		
7.	Which is greater, $\frac{1}{8}$ of 96 or $\frac{2}{7}$ of 35?		
8.	Which is greater, $\frac{4}{5}$ of 60 or $\frac{4}{7}$ of 98?		
9.	Which is greater, $\frac{4}{5}$ of 50 or $\frac{1}{10}$ of 200?		
10.	Which is greater, $\frac{2}{3}$ of 30 or $\frac{2}{9}$ of 81?		

Go Further

11. Write three of your own *Which is Greater* problems. For one of them, make sure the answer is *neither*. Ask a friend to solve your problems.

_____

_____

_____

Friend's name _____

12. If $\frac{2}{3}$ of some number is eight, how can you find $\frac{3}{4}$ of the same number?

_____

_____

_____

On today's activity: (Circle one) I need to know more. I got it.

Name

Date

121

Today's Challenge ✎ Rolling Sums

Two events are said to be *equally likely* if they have the same chance of happening. *Experimental probability* is based on data you've collected.

If you roll a cube and your partner rolls a different cube, then *you: 3, friend: 6* is a different result than *you: 6, friend: 3*.

1. In how many different ways could you roll your two number cubes to obtain a sum of three? List all the ways.

   _____

2. In how many ways could you and your partner roll a sum of eight? List all the ways.

   _____

3. Based on this information, do you think you have the same chance of rolling a sum of three as a sum of eight? Explain.

   _____

Work with a partner. Roll two number cubes 50 times, keeping track of the sum of each roll on this line plot.

_____

2 3 4 5 6 7 8 9 10 11 12

4. Was your answer to exercise 3 proved true in your experiment? Why do you think this is so?

   _____

5. What sum(s) are you most likely to get if you do another trial? _____

6. What sum(s) are you least likely to get if you do another trial? _____

7. What is the experimental probability of rolling a sum of six? _____

8. What is the experimental probability of rolling a sum of 11? _____

9. What is the experimental probability of rolling a sum greater than four? _____

10. What is the experimental probability of rolling a sum that is even? _____

11. What is the experimental probability of rolling a sum of 13? _____

On today's activity: (Circle one) ✎ I need to know more. ✎ I got it.

Go Further   Rolling Sums

Work with your partner and do more trials like those on page 122 until you have data from 100 rolls. Keep track any way you like. Study and analyze your results and record your observations here or on another piece of paper.

Things we discovered: _____

When you find probabilities from a table like this one, based on theory, you are finding *theoretical probability*.

1. Create a *sample space* for rolling your two number cubes. Fill in sums of possible rolls.

Cube 1

+	1	2	3	4	5	6
1						
2						
3						
4						
5						
6						

Cube 2

2. According to the table, what should be the most common outcome? _____

3. How many possible outcomes are there? _____

4. Write as a fraction the theoretical probability of rolling each sum.

   a. 4 _____   b. 7 _____   c. 12 _____   d. 1 _____

5. Should you be more likely to roll a sum of six or a sum of three? Explain.

   _____

6. How does the theoretical probability of rolling these sums match with the results of your experiment?

   _____

7. Why do you think that experimental probability does not always match theoretical probability?

   _____

On today's activity: (Circle one)   I need to know more.   I got it.

Name   **Date**   123

Get Started

One Pound

$\frac{1}{16}$ lb or 1 oz	$\frac{1}{16}$ lb or 1 oz	$\frac{1}{16}$ lb or 1 oz	$\frac{1}{16}$ lb or 1 oz	$\frac{1}{16}$ lb or 1 oz	$\frac{1}{16}$ lb or 1 oz	$\frac{1}{16}$ lb or 1 oz	$\frac{1}{16}$ lb or 1 oz
$\frac{1}{16}$ lb or 1 oz	$\frac{1}{16}$ lb or 1 oz	$\frac{1}{16}$ lb or 1 oz	$\frac{1}{16}$ lb or 1 oz	$\frac{1}{16}$ lb or 1 oz	$\frac{1}{16}$ lb or 1 oz	$\frac{1}{16}$ lb or 1 oz	$\frac{1}{16}$ lb or 1 oz

Today's Challenge **Complete the table.** Write fractions in simplest form.

1. 4 ounces _____

2. $\frac{3}{8}$ pound _____

3. _____ 12 ounces

4. $\frac{5}{16}$ pound _____

5. 2 ounces _____

6. _____ $\frac{1}{16}$ pound

7. _____ 14 ounces

8. $\frac{5}{8}$ pound _____

9. 20 ounces _____

10. $\frac{1}{2}$ pound _____

On today's activity: (Circle one) I need to know more. I got it.

Get Started 🖊 Fill in the letter of the correct answer.

Which of these examples shows a way to find 20% of 84? Explain
why each choice will or will not work, then find its value.

(A) 0.2×84 _____

(B) $84 \div 0.2$ _____

(C) $84 \div \frac{1}{5}$ _____

Today's Challenge 🖊 Fill in the letter of the correct computation method.

Decide whether to use a calculator, mental math, or paper and pencil. Then,
write each product.

1. The cost of a dress at this sale.

   (A) $0.25 \times \$72.00$ _____

   (B) $0.75 \times \$72.00$ _____

   (C) $\frac{1}{4} \times \$72.00$ _____

DEBBIE'S DRESSES
Original Price: $72.00
Sale: 25% off

2. The cost of a baseball glove at this sale.

   (A) $\frac{6}{10} \times \$52.00$ _____

   (B) $\frac{4}{10} \times \$52.00$ _____

   (C) $1.4 \times \$52.00$ _____

SALE!
Baseball gloves
Original Price: $52.00
Sale: 40% off

3. The price of a new pair of this year's skates.

   (A) $\$85.00 - (0.3 \times \$85.00)$ _____

   (B) $0.3 \times \$85.00$ _____

   (C) $\$85.00 + (0.3 \times \$85.00)$ _____

Skates
Last year's models $85.00
This year's models 30% more

4. For which expressions in exercises 1–3 was mental math faster
   than using a calculator? Write the letters of the expressions. _____

5. What advice would you give to a student about computing the percent of
   a given number?

   _____

   _____

   _____

   _____

On today's activity: (Circle one) 🖊 I need to know more. ▪ I got it.

Name _____   Date _____   125

Today's Challenge 🔷 Fill in the rest of the table.

Figure	Dimensions	Area	Perimeter
Rectangle	1. length: width:	154 square centimeters	2.
Square	3. length: width:	4.	32 inches
Rectangle	5. length: width:	117 square feet	44 feet
Square	6. length: width:	81 square yards	7.
Rectangle	8. length: width:	180 square feet	9.
Square	10. length: width:	100 square feet	11.
Rectangle	length: 10 inches width: 2 inches	12.	13.
Rectangle	14. length: width:	80 square yards	48 yards

Go Further

15. Find three possible perimeters for a rectangle with an area of 16 square feet.
Use whole-number units.

_____

16. Relate your answer to exercise 15 to the factors for 16.

_____

17. Find four possible areas for a rectangle with a perimeter of 16 feet.
Use whole-number units.

_____

18. Do you think there could be more than four answers to exercise 17? Explain.

_____

On today's activity: (Circle one) 🔷 I need to know more. 🔷 I got it.

Date

Today's Challenge   The Match Me Challenge

Work with a partner and play the *Match Me* game. If your last name is first in alphabetical order, you are Player A. Otherwise, you are Player B. Each Player will flip a coin. If the two coins match (heads-heads or tails-tails), then Player A wins. If the two coins do not match (heads-tails or tails-heads), then Player B wins. Play the game 50 times and record the results in the table.

	Tallies	Total
Player A (match)		
Player B (no match)		

1. Based on the table, what is the experimental probability that two flipped coins will come up heads-heads or tails-tails? _____

2. Based on the table, what is the experimental probability that two flipped coils will come up heads-tails or tails-heads? _____

3. What is the sum of the two probabilities in exercises 1 and 2? _____

4. Get the totals from the fifty trials of three other groups and show your results in a double bar graph. Bar A will show Player A's wins. Bar B will show Player B's wins. The last pair of bars should show the mean of the four sets of data.

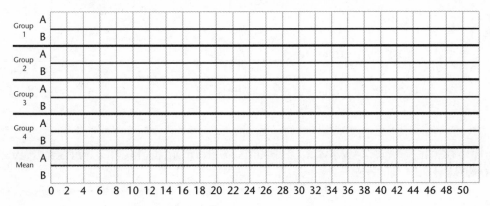

5. A game is said to be *fair* if both players are equally likely to win the game. Based on your graph, do you think this is a fair game?

Explain. _____

_____

On today's activity: (Circle one)   I need to know more.   I got it.

Name   **Date**   127

Go Further   The Match Me Challenge

Work with your partner to study your work on page 127 and the
tree diagram showing the sample space for flipping two coins.
Write what you've discovered about the fairness of flipping two coins.

Things we discovered: _____

_____

_____

Coin 1   Coin 2
Two-Coin Toss

Suppose that a coin-flipping game requires two players and three coins.

1. Complete the sample space to show all the possible outcomes.

Three-Coin Toss

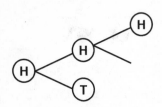

2. What are the possible outcomes? _____

3. Are all the outcomes equally likely? Explain. _____

_____

4. For this game, Player A wins if the coins match, and Player B wins if they do not
   match. Is this a fair game? Explain.

_____

_____

5. If the game in exercise 4 is not fair, how could you make it fair?

_____

_____

On today's activity: (Circle one)   I need to know more.   I got it.

Date

Today's Challenge Look for two-digit numbers that, when multiplied by $\frac{1}{2}$, $\frac{1}{3}$, or $\frac{1}{4}$ equal **whole numbers.** Write the facts you find in word form and symbolic form.

Example: one-half of 36 is 18; $\frac{1}{2} \times 36 = 18$

one half of _____ is _____; $\frac{1}{2} \times$ _____ = _____

one half of _____ is _____; $\frac{1}{2} \times$ _____ = _____

one half of _____ is _____; $\frac{1}{2} \times$ _____ = _____

one third of _____ is _____; $\frac{1}{3} \times$ _____ = _____

one third of _____ is _____; $\frac{1}{3} \times$ _____ = _____

one third of _____ is _____; $\frac{1}{3} \times$ _____ = _____

one fourth of _____ is _____; $\frac{1}{4} \times$ _____ = _____

one fourth of _____ is _____; $\frac{1}{4} \times$ _____ = _____

one fourth of _____ is _____; $\frac{1}{4} \times$ _____ = _____

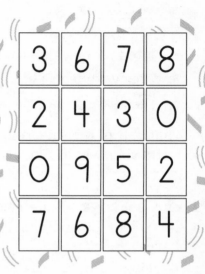

Go Further Create your own **Math Jumble.** Include two-digit numbers that, when multiplied by $\frac{1}{2}$, $\frac{1}{3}$, or $\frac{1}{4}$ equal whole numbers. Include two of each type. Have a friend use your Math Jumble to find your six facts. Have your friend write the facts. If you disagree on the facts or their products, check your work. Edit if necessary.

1. one half of _____ is _____; $\frac{1}{2} \times$ _____ = _____

2. one half of _____ is _____; $\frac{1}{2} \times$ _____ = _____

3. one third of _____ is _____; $\frac{1}{3} \times$ _____ = _____

4. one third of _____ is _____; $\frac{1}{3} \times$ _____ = _____

5. one fourth of _____ is _____; $\frac{1}{4} \times$ _____ = _____

6. one fourth of _____ is _____; $\frac{1}{4} \times$ _____ = _____

Friend's name _____

On today's activity: (Circle one) I need to know more. I got it.

Name

Date

Get Started ✏ **Refer to the table.** Fill in the appropriate response grid.

Favorite-Flavor Ice Cream Survey: Gauss Middle School

Flavor	Chocolate	Vanilla	Strawberry	Black Raspberry
Number of Students	8	5	7	4

Students voted for only one flavor.

A. **B.** **C.**

(A) How many students participated in the survey?

(B) What fraction of the students liked chocolate best?

(C) What part of the students liked vanilla or strawberry best? Show your response as a decimal.

Today's Challenge ✏ **Refer to the table.** Show your work, then fill in the appropriate response grid.

Crude Oil Production, 2000

Country	Qatar	Iran	Saudi Arabia	Venezuela	Iraq	Indonesia	Nigeria
Barrels per day	737,000	3,719,000	8,404,000	2,949,000	2,571,000	1,466,000	2,144,000

(Source: www.eia.doe.gov/emeu/ipsr/+41a.txt)

1. **2.** **3.**

1. Of the countries in the table, how many produced between two million and four million barrels per day?

2. Iran, Iraq, Indonesia, and Nigeria produced about how many millions of barrels of crude oil per day in 2000?

3. Use front-end estimation. About what part of Nigeria's production is Indonesia's production? Show your response as a decimal.

4. What advice would you give a student estimating with large numbers?

_____

_____

_____

On today's activity: (Circle one) ✏ I need to know more. ✏ I got it.

130 **Name**

Date

Today's Challenge Use mental math to fill in the table. You will find a percent of each dollar amount. If your calculations are correct, the sum of your answers will be $100!

Go Further

11. Make your own set of 10 percent problems. The sum of your answers should be $50. Give them to a friend to solve.

	Percent	Amount	Answer
1.	10%	$18.40	
2.	50%	$38.60	
3.	25%	$28.40	
4.	$33\frac{1}{3}$%	$6.30	
5.	10%	$42.50	
6.	25%	$48.80	
7.	$33\frac{1}{3}$%	$39.90	
8.	50%	$46.80	
9.	25%	$60.00	
10.	10%	$15.10	
			$100.00

Percent	Amount	Answer
		$50.00

Friend's name

_____

12. It is common to leave a 15% tip for the server at a restaurant. Your dinner bill is $48.35. Explain how to approximate a 15% tip.

_____

_____

_____

On today's activity: (Circle one) I need to know more. I got it.

Name

Date

Today's Challenge ✎ Roll a Number

Work with a partner. One partner takes a number cube and the other partner keeps track of the number of rolls it takes before a four comes up. Take turns and do this experiment 20 times.

Trial	1	2	3	4	5	6	7	8	9	10
Rolls to Get 4										
Trial	11	12	13	14	15	16	17	18	19	20
Rolls to Get 4										

1. Find the mean number of times you needed to roll the cube to have it land four-up. _____

2. How do you think your answer to exercise 1 would change if you were looking for ones instead of fours?

   _____

3. What was the experimental probability of rolling a four on the first roll? (Remember: the number of trials was 20, so your answer should be a fraction with 20 in the denominator.) _____

4. What was the experimental probability of *not* rolling a four on the first roll?

   _____

5. What was the experimental probability of rolling a four before the fourth roll?

   _____

6. What was the experimental probability of *not* rolling a four on any of the first three rolls?

   _____

On today's activity: (Circle one) ✎ I need to know more. ▊ I got it.

Date

Go Further — Roll a Number

Work with your partner. Put your results from page 132 on this line plot. Then, do 20 more trials, recording the results on the same line plot. Study your line plot and write any patterns or other interesting facts you discover.

Line Plot: Rolls to Get Four

1 2 3 4 5 6 7 8 9 10 11 12 13 14 15
Number of Rolls

Things we discovered: _____

_____

_____

_____

_____

1. Find the mean of the number of rolls it took to get a four. _____

2. What was the experimental probability of rolling a four on the first roll? _____

3. What was the experimental probability of *not* rolling a four on the first roll? _____

4. What was the experimental probability of rolling a four on any of the first three rolls? _____

5. What was the experimental probability of *not* rolling a four on any of the first three rolls? _____

6. How are your answers to exercises 2–5 different from your answers to exercises 3–6 on page 132? (Consider simplifying your fractions.) Explain.

_____

_____

_____

On today's activity: (Circle one) — I need to know more. — I got it.

Name

Date

133

Go Further 🖉 Follow the directions to mark numbers in the grid.
Some numbers will be marked more than once.

1. Cross out all numbers that are equal to the number of inches in $\frac{1}{2}$ foot or in $\frac{1}{2}$ yard.

1	2	3	4	5	6	7	8	9	10	11	12
13	14	15	16	17	18	19	20	21	22	23	24
25	26	27	28	29	30	31	32	33	34	35	36

2. Star all numbers that are less than the number of inches in $\frac{2}{3}$ foot.

3. Circle all numbers that are greater than or equal to the number of inches in $2\frac{1}{4}$ feet.

4. Box all numbers that are even.

5. Underline all numbers that are less than the number of inches in two feet.

6. Which number is not marked? _____

7. Create your own "Fantastic Finalist" activity for a friend to solve. If you disagree on the answer, recheck your work and edit if you need to.

1	2	3	4	5	6	7	8	9	10	11	12
13	14	15	16	17	18	19	20	21	22	23	24
25	26	27	28	29	30	31	32	33	34	35	36

- _____ all numbers that are _____.
- _____ all numbers that are _____.
- _____ all numbers that are _____.
- _____ all numbers that are _____.
- _____ all numbers that are _____.
- _____ all numbers that are _____.

Friend's name _____

On today's activity: (Circle one) 🖉 I need to know more. 🖉 I got it.

Date

Get Started 〰 **Fill in the circle of the correct answer.**

Refer to the line plot, histogram, and bar graph.

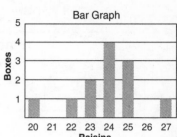

Line Plot
Raisins per Box

(A) How many boxes have
between 21 and 25 raisins? _____

(B) How many boxes of raisins
were used in this study? _____

(C) What was the greatest number of
raisins found in any of the boxes? _____

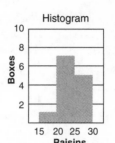

Histogram

Bar Graph

(D) About what percent of the boxes
had either 23 or 24 raisins? _____

(E) Which graph was most useful for answering questions A–D? Explain.

_____

Today's Challenge 〰 **Fill in the circle of the correct
response.** Refer to the line plot to help you answer
exercises 1–4.

Pets Owned by Classmates

1. How many students are there in the class?

   (A) 16   (B) 20   (C) 40   (D) 7

2. How many pets are owned by students in the class?

   (A) 16   (B) 20   (C) 40   (D) 7

3. What was the mode for the number of pets owned by the classmates?

   (A) 8   (B) 7   (C) 4   (D) 1

4. What was the median number of pets owned by students in the class?

   (A) 1   (B) 1.5   (C) 2   (D) 2.5

5. Draw a bar graph and a histogram to show the data in the line plot.

6. What advice would you give to a student who is graphing data from a survey?

_____

_____

On today's activity: (Circle one) 〰 I need to know more. 〰 I got it.

Name

Date

Today's Challenge — Fill in the table.

Examples: • $\frac{2}{6}$ of a foot is 4 inches

• $\frac{1}{5}$ of a dollar is 20 cents

• $\frac{1}{2}$ hour is 30 minutes.

□	Inches in □ Foot	Ounces in □ Pound	Hours in □ Day	Minutes in □ Hour	Cents in □ Dollar
$\frac{1}{2}$	1.	2.	3.	4.	5.
$\frac{2}{3}$	6.		7.	8.	
$\frac{3}{4}$	9.	10.	11.	12.	13.
$\frac{1}{4}$	14.	15.	16.	17.	18.
$\frac{1}{8}$		19.	20.		
$\frac{1}{6}$	21.		22.	23.	
$\frac{2}{5}$				24.	25.
$\frac{1}{3}$	26.		27.	28.	
$\frac{5}{6}$	29.		30.	31.	

32. Why do you think some cells in the table are shaded? _____

_____

_____

Go Further — There are 5280 feet in one mile.

33. How many feet are in $\frac{1}{2}$ mile? _____   **34.** How many feet are in $\frac{2}{3}$ mile? _____

35. How many feet are in $\frac{3}{4}$ mile? _____   **36.** How many feet are in $\frac{1}{4}$ mile? _____

37. How many feet are in $\frac{1}{8}$ mile? _____   **38.** How many feet are in $\frac{1}{6}$ mile? _____

39. How many feet are in $\frac{2}{5}$ mile? _____   **40.** How many feet are in $\frac{1}{3}$ mile? _____

41. How many feet are in $\frac{5}{6}$ mile? _____

On today's activity: (Circle one) — I need to know more. — I got it.

Date

Today's Challenge — Multiplication by Three and Seven and Their Stars

There are many interesting patterns which arise when you multiply by certain numbers. Today you will collect data about multiples of three and of seven.

1. 0 ×3	2. 1 ×3	3. 2 ×3	4. 3 ×3	5. 4 ×3
6. 5 ×3	7. 6 ×3	8. 7 ×3	9. 8 ×3	10. 9 ×3
11. 10 ×3	12. 11 ×3	13. 12 ×3	14. 13 ×3	15. 14 ×3
16. 15 ×3	17. 16 ×3	18. 17 ×3	19. 18 ×3	20. 19 ×3
21. 0 ×7	22. 1 ×7	23. 2 ×7	24. 3 ×7	25. 4 ×7
26. 5 ×7	27. 6 ×7	28. 7 ×7	29. 8 ×7	30. 9 ×7
31. 10 ×7	32. 11 ×7	33. 12 ×7	34. 13 ×7	35. 14 ×7
36. 15 ×7	37. 16 ×7	38. 17 ×7	39. 18 ×7	40. 19 ×7

On today's activity: (Circle one) — I need to know more. — I got it.

Name

Date

137

Go Further 〜 Multiplication by Three and Seven and Their Stars

Work with a partner to study the products on page 137. Write your observations here or on a separate sheet of paper.

Things we discovered: _____

_____

_____

_____

_____

_____

1. Write the pattern in the ones digits in the multiples of three. _____

2. Write the pattern in the ones digits in the multiples of seven. _____

3. Examine these circles.
   • In the first circle, start at zero.
   • In order, draw line segments to the ones digits in the products of three and the numbers 30 through 40.
   • In the second circle, connect the ones digits of the products of seven and the numbers 30 through 40.

   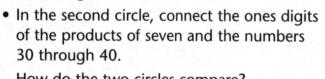

   How do the two circles compare? _____

4. Did you need to compute the multiples of three and seven for exercise 3? _____ If yes, edit your answers to exercises 1 and 2.

5. If you multiply 43 by each of the numbers 21 through 30, does the pattern you discovered still predict the ones digits of your products? Explain.

   _____

   _____

   _____

On today's activity: (Circle one) 〜 I need to know more. 〜 I got it.

Get Started

1. Complete the table.

+	3	5	6
⁻2			
⁻4			
⁻8			

Go Further ✏ **Solve the riddles.**

2. **Clues:** • I have a sum of ⁻9.

   • One of my addends is ⁻4.

   What is my other addend? _____

3. **Clues:** • I have a sum of 4.

   • One of my addends is ⁻5.

   What is my other addend? _____

4. Fill in the blanks to make and solve a riddle.

   Clues: • I have a sum of _____

   • One of my addends is _____

   What is my other addend? _____

5. Now write your own riddle for a friend to solve.

   Clues: _____

   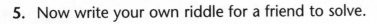

   _____

   _____

   _____

   _____

   What is my other addend? _____

   Friend's name _____

On today's activity: (Circle one) ✏ I need to know more. ✏ I got it.

Name   **Date**

Get Started
Refer to the graph to answer the questions.

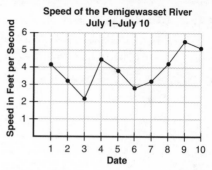

Speed of the Pemigewasset River
July 1–July 10

(A) What was the fastest speed recorded during the ten days? _____

(B) When did the speed increase the most and how great was the increase?

_____

(C) What was the slowest speed recorded in the ten days? _____

Today's Challenge
Refer to the graphs to answer the questions.

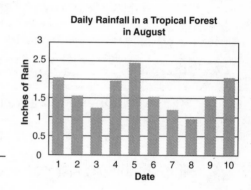

Daily Rainfall in a Tropical Forest in August

1. On which day did the most rain fall? _____

2. What day had the least rain and how much rain fell that day? _____

3. What percent of days received 1.5 inches or more of rain? _____

4. What was the greatest decrease in rainfall from one day to the next and when did it occur? _____

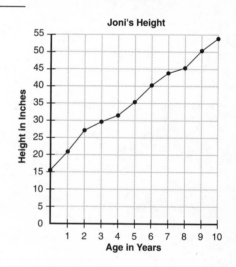

Joni's Height

5. About how much did Joni grow from age two to age five? _____

6. How tall was Joni at age six? _____

7. About how much did Joni grow from birth to age two? _____

8. Over what two-year period did Joni's growth slow down? _____

9. What was the average (mean) growth per year for the ten years? _____

10. What advice would you give to a student who is reading graphs?

_____

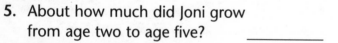

_____

_____

On today's activity: (Circle one) I need to know more. I got it.

140 Name _____

Date _____

Today's Challenge Put parentheses around the first operation you should do, according to the order of operations. Then compute.

1. $7 + 3 \times 8 =$ _____

2. $10^2 - 22 =$ _____

3. $6 \times 5 + 6 =$ _____

4. $10 + 8^2 =$ _____

5. $5 + 2 \times 7 =$ _____

6. $5 \times 5 - 25 =$ _____

7. $4 \times 5 \div 2 =$ _____

8. $48 \div 6 \times 7 =$ _____

9. $34 - 18 + 12 =$ _____

10. $9 \times 5 - 20 =$ _____

11. $4 + 9 \times 9 =$ _____

12. $16 + 10^2 - 86 =$ _____

13. $2 + 8 \times 8 =$ _____

14. $3 \times 4^2 - 35 =$ _____

15. $54 \div 9 \times 3 =$ _____

Go Further Insert parentheses to make each equation true.

16. $18 + 9 \div 3 + 20 = 29$

17. $9 \times 4 - 2 = 18$

18. $6 + 3 \times 8 - 3 = 45$

19. Make up four of your own problems using order of operations rules. Ask a friend to solve them.

_____

_____

_____

_____

Friend's name _____

On today's activity: (Circle one) I need to know more. I got it.

Name   **Date**   141

Today's Challenge — Going Around in Circles

The *circumference* of a circle is the distance around it. A *diameter* of a circle is a line segment that passes through the center of the circle and has endpoints on the circle. (It is the *longest* segment with endpoints on a circle.) Work with a partner. Use string and a centimeter ruler to make your measurements.

1. Find the lengths of the circumferences and diameters for five circular objects. Record your findings in the table. Use a calculator to find the ratio of the circumference to the diameter in each of the circular objects you measured. Record the ratio as a decimal rounded to the nearest tenth.

Object					
Circumference (in centimeters)					
Diameter (in centimeters)					
Ratio of Circumference to Diameter					

2. Get the data from one other pair of students and use it to fill in this chart.

Object					
Circumference (in centimeters)					
Diameter (in centimeters)					
Ratio of Circumference to Diameter					

On today's activity: (Circle one) — I need to know more. — I got it.

Name

Date

Go Further — **Going Around in Circles**

Work with your partner. Examine the data on page 142 to see what relationships you can discover. Record your discoveries here or an another piece of paper.

Things we discovered: _____

_____

_____

_____

_____

Use the tables on page 142 and your list of discoveries to answer these questions.

1. What happens to the circumference when the diameter increases? _____

_____

2. Compare the ten ratios. _____

3. What is the mean for the ten ratios? _____

4. The diameter of a circle is 24 centimeters. Based on what you have discovered, predict the circumference for that circle. Explain.

_____

_____

5. Predict the length of the diameter for a circle whose circumference is 38 centimeters. Explain your reasoning.

_____

_____

6. If you read a report that said a circle had a circumference of 48 centimeters and a diameter of a little less than 8 centimeters, what would you say about that report?

_____

_____

On today's activity: (Circle one) — I need to know more. — I got it.

Name _____ **Date** _____

Get Started All quadrilaterals on this page are rectangles.

Example 1		Example 2	
Area: 10 square centimeters	2 cm __5__ cm	Area: 10 square centimeters	1 cm __10__ cm

Today's Challenge Fill in the table.

1. Area: 24 square centimeters	2 cm _____ cm	2. Area: 24 square centimeters	_____ cm 6 cm
3. Area: 24 square yards	3 yd _____ yd	4. Area: 24 square yards	1 yd _____ yd
5. Area: 28 square inches	4 in. _____ in.	6. Area: 28 square inches	2 in. _____ in.
7. Area: 28 square kilometers	___ km 28 km	8. Area: 28 square kilometers	___ km 7 km
9. Area: 30 square feet	5 ft _____ ft	10. Area: 30 square feet	_____ ft 10 ft
11. Area: 30 square millimeters	2 mm _____ mm	12. Area: 30 square millimeters	1 mm _____ mm
13. Area: 36 square miles	___ mi 9 mi	14. Area: 36 square miles	___ mi 18 mi
15. Area: 36 square feet	3 ft _____ ft	16. Area: 36 square feet	6 ft ___ ft

On today's activity: (Circle one) I need to know more. I got it.

144 Name

Date

Get Started — **Rule out two answer choices.** Explain why you eliminated each of these choices. Then fill in the circle of the correct answer.

Heidi ate a meal at a restaurant. The total bill was $15.75. About how much should she leave for a 15% tip?

(A) $18.00 _____

(B) $2.50 _____

(C) $0.25 _____

(D) $19.50 _____

How did you choose the correct answer from the remaining two?

_____

Today's Challenge — **Rule out two answer choices.** Explain why you eliminated each of these choices. Then fill in the circle of the correct answer.

1. Heidi went shopping after her meal. She bought a CD that cost $12.99. The sales tax in her state is 7%. How much did she pay for tax on her new CD?

(A) $14.69 _____

(B) $13.90 _____

(C) $9.10 _____

(D) $0.91 _____

How did you choose the correct answer from the remaining two?

_____

2. Heidi's taxi ride home cost $10.25. She wants to give the driver a tip of about 15%, but she does not want to search for coins. How much should she give the driver?

(A) $12.00 _____

(B) $15.00 _____

(C) $11.00 _____

(D) $13.00 _____

How did you choose the correct answer from the remaining two?

_____

3. What advice would you give to a student taking a test on percent?

_____

_____

_____

_____

On today's activity: (Circle one) — I need to know more. — I got it.

Name **Date** 145

Today's Challenge — Find the value of each expression.

1. What is the value of $2x + 3$ if $x = 9$? _____

2. What is the value of $x + 15$ if $x = 12$? _____

3. What is the value of $6x - 1$ if $x = 5$? _____

4. What is the value of $9 + 3x$ if $x = 7$? _____

5. What is the value of $4 + x^2$ if $x = 3$? _____

6. What is the value of $x \div 4 + 5$ if $x = 16$? _____

7. What is the value of $7(x - 3)$ if $x = 8$? _____

8. What is the value of $8 + \frac{x}{3}$ if $x = 6$? _____

9. What is the value of $x^2 - 41$ if $x = 7$? _____

10. What is the value of $37 - 5x$ if $x = 3$? _____

Go Further

11. Find the value of the expression $5x - 4$ when the value for x changes.
    Record your answers in the table.

Expression	Value of x	Value of Expression
$5x - 4$	2	
$5x - 4$	3	
$5x - 4$	4	
$5x - 4$	5	

12. What pattern do you see in your answers to exercise 11? Explain the pattern.

    _____

13. Write an expression whose value will increase by 10 when the value
    of x increases by one.

    _____

On today's activity: (Circle one) I need to know more. I got it.

Date

Today's Challenge How Many Degrees?

Work with a partner. Take turns using the protractor to find the measures of the angles in the figures. Write the angle measures and their sum in each figure.

1.
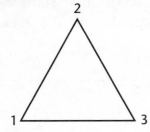

2.
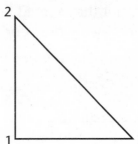

3.
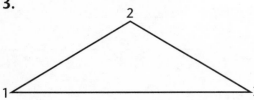

4.
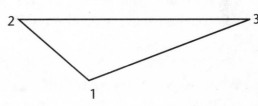

5.
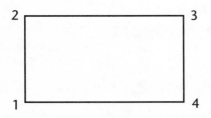

6.
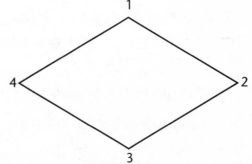

7.
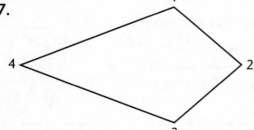

8.
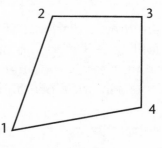

On today's activity: (Circle one) I need to know more. I got it.

Name

Date

Go Further How Many Degrees?

Work with your partner. Compare your angle-sums on page 147 with another pair of students. If there are any large discrepancies, check to see if you made a mistake. Because measurement is always inaccurate, you should not expect the sums to be exactly the same, but they should be close to one another. Study angle-sums for each type of figure, then write your discoveries here or on another piece of paper.

Things we discovered: _____

_____

_____

1. What do you think might be true about the
   sum of the measures of the angles in any triangle? _____

   _____

2. What do you think might be true about the sum
   of the measures of the angles in any quadrilateral? _____

   _____

3. If the sum of the measures of two angles of a triangle is
   141°, what is the measure of the third angle in the triangle? _____

4. If the sum of the measures of three angles of a
   quadrilateral is 312°, what is the measure of the fourth angle? _____

5. What relationship do you see between the angle-sums
   of a triangle and the angle-sums of a quadrilateral? _____

   _____

6. When you draw a diagonal of a quadrilateral, you can see that
   the quadrilateral is made up of two triangles. If you do the same
   thing for a pentagon, you get three triangles. What do you think
   is the angle-sum for a pentagon? Explain your reasoning.

   _____

   _____

On today's activity: (Circle one) I need to know more. I got it.

Date

Today's Challenge ◢ **Look for strings of digits that could be used to make number patterns.** The pattern should include at least four numbers. Write the number patterns. Then write the next three numbers that appear in the pattern.

1	3	5	0
5	6	7	8
2	9	1	2
3	6	1	4

Number pattern

_____

_____

_____

_____

_____

Next three numbers

_____

_____

_____

_____

_____

Go Further ◢ **Create your own Math Jumble.** Include the first four numbers of three different number patterns. Have a friend use your Math Jumble to find the three number patterns and the next three numbers in each one. If you disagree, check your work. Edit if necessary.

Number pattern

_____

_____

_____

_____

_____

Next three numbers

_____

_____

_____

_____

_____

Friend's name _____

On today's activity: (Circle one) ◢ I need to know more. ◢ I got it.

Name

Date

149

Get Started 　 Study the problem and complete the constructed response.

Problem: Start with your age in years. Multiply by six. Add 18 to the product. Divide the sum by six. Subtract three from the quotient. The difference should be your age. Why does this work no matter what your age?

Solution:

First, write the steps as a mathematical expression. Let your age be **A.** _____	$(x \cdot 6 + 18) \div 6 - 3$ $\downarrow$ $\frac{6x + 18}{6} - 3$
Next, use the Distributive Property to make the expression simpler.	$\frac{6x}{6} + \frac{18}{6} - 3$ $\downarrow$ $x + 3 - 3)$ $\downarrow$ **B.** _____
Finally, answer the question in the problem.	In this problem, you multiply your age by six, then add 18, which is also divisible by six. Then, when you divide by six, you get your age ($6x \div 6 = x$) plus three ($18 \div 6 = 3$). The final step, **C.** _____, gets you back to your age by getting rid of the number that's left after dividing **D.** _____.

Today's Challenge 　 Write a constructed response on a separate sheet of paper.

1. **Problem:** Pick a number between two and ten. If the number is odd, add one. Divide by two. If the quotient is odd, subtract one. Your result is an even number. What numbers could you have started with in order to end up with two?

2. What advice do you have for someone designing number puzzles?

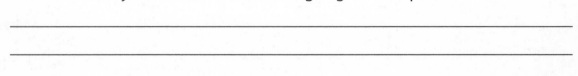

_____

_____

_____

On today's activity: (Circle one) 　 I need to know more. 　 I got it.

150 **Name**

Date

Today's Challenge Fill in the blanks in this table to show values represented in equivalent forms. Write all fractions in simplest form.

	Fraction	Decimal	Percent
1.			40%
2.		0.25	
3.	$\frac{3}{8}$		
4.			$33\frac{1}{3}\%$
5.		0.5	
6.	$\frac{3}{10}$		
7.			20%
8.	$\frac{4}{5}$		
9.		0.45	
10.			75%

Go Further

11. Write these fractions, decimals, and percents in order from least to greatest.

	$\frac{2}{5}$	
20%		0.95
	$\frac{1}{3}$	
60%		0.02
	$\frac{1}{8}$	
85%		0.45
	$\frac{7}{10}$	

On today's activity: (Circle one)   I need to know more.   I got it.

Name _____   **Date** _____   **151**

Today's Challenge Numbers as Shapes

Work with a partner. Use your colored squares to form as many different rectangles with the given area as possible. Keep good records in the table. The first is done for you. Notice that a 6 × 1 rectangle is *not* different from a 1 × 6 rectangle.

Same Area
Same Rectangle

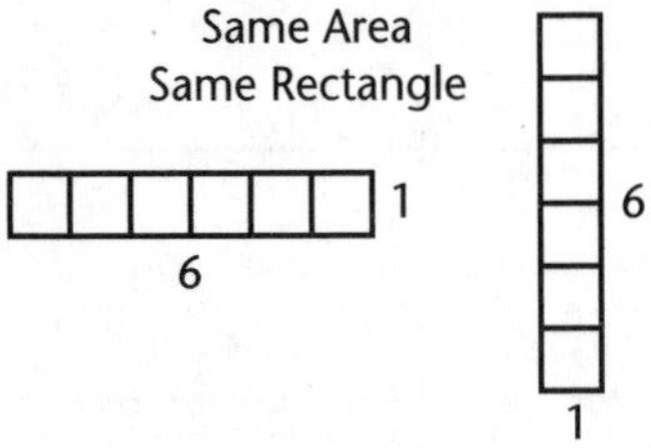

6

1

6

1

Same Area
Different Rectangle

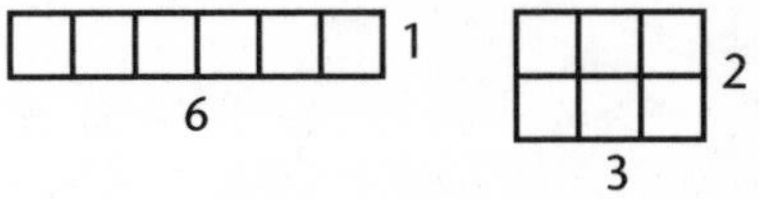

6

1

2

3

Area (in squares)	Dimensions of Rectangle (in units)	Number of Different Side Lengths
6	1 × 6, 2 × 3	4
7		
8		
9		
10		
11		
12		
16		
20		
21		
22		
23		
24		
25		

On today's activity: (Circle one) I need to know more. I got it.

152 **Name**   **Date**

Go Further — Numbers as Shapes

Work with your partner. Study the data from the table on page 152. Write any patterns or interesting facts you notice here or on another piece of paper.

Things we discovered: _____

_____

In mathematics, the relationships between some numbers in a group can many times be true for all the numbers in the group.

1. Compare the number of different side-lengths for each rectangle to the factors of its area. _____

2. Sort each number from the area column on page 152 into this table.

3. What is true about rectangles whose areas are prime numbers?

_____

_____

_____

_____

Exactly Two Factors	Odd Number of Factors	Even Number of Factors(> 2)

4. Why do you think square numbers are called that? Give an example in your explanation.

_____

_____

_____

5. Name at least two differences between square and composite numbers.

_____

_____

On today's activity: (Circle one) — I need to know more. — I got it.

Name _____ **Date** _____

153

Go Further — Follow the directions to mark numbers in the grid. Some numbers will be marked more than once.

324	732	408	330
61	49	564	134
345	644	360	36
252	938	693	828

1. Cross out all numbers that are divisible by seven.

2. Star all numbers that are divisible by five.

3. Circle all numbers that are divisible by three.

4. Underline all numbers that are divisible by four.

5. Shade the squares containing numbers that are divisible by two.

6. Which number is not marked? _____

7. Is the answer to exercise 6 divisible by ten? How do you know?

_____

_____

8. Is the answer to exercise 6 divisible by six? How do you know?

_____

_____

9. What name is given to the type of number you did not mark? _____

On today's activity: (Circle one) — I need to know more. — I got it.

Get Started Here are four examples of June's work on a test of her ability to find circumference. Mark the letter of each problem that June has solved correctly, then correct her mistakes.

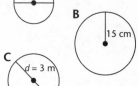

(A) C = 10π inches _____

(B) C = 15π centimeters _____

(C) C = 3π meters _____

(D) C = 5π feet _____

Today's Challenge

1. For which of these circles do you think June would find the correct circumference? Explain, then find the correct circumference.

(A) _____

(B) _____

(C) _____

(D) _____

2. Redraw these diagrams so that June can find the correct circumference, then find the circumference.

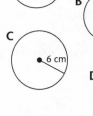

(A) _____

(B) _____

(C) _____

(D) _____

3. What advice would you give June about finding the circumference of a circle?

_____

_____

On today's activity: (Circle one) I need to know more. I got it.

Name _____ Date _____ **155**

Week 31•Activity 155

Today's Challenge Circle the expression with greater value, then write the difference between the two values.

1. $\frac{7}{8}$ of 80 or 9×10 _____

2. $3 \times 10 \times 10 \times 10$ or 1000 _____

3. $\frac{5}{6}$ or 0.5 _____

4. 0.5×200 or $\frac{1}{2}$ of 300 _____

5. $\frac{1}{3}$ or $\frac{35}{100}$ _____

6. $\frac{3}{8}$ of 16 or 10% of 120 _____

7. 9^2 or 10^2 _____

8. $2100 \div 70$ or $\frac{1}{2}$ of 70 _____

9. 0.7 or 0.07 _____

10. 0.8×80 or $\frac{1}{8}$ of 80 _____

Write the correct comparison, using the symbols >, <, and =.

11. $\frac{1}{10}$ of 150 ☐ $\frac{1}{2}$ of 30

12. 4^2 ☐ 5×3

13. $\frac{1}{4}$ ☐ 0.2

14. four tenths ☐ fourteen hundredths

15. $7\frac{1}{2}$ ☐ 7.05

16. 60×8 ☐ 80×6

17. $2^2 \times 3$ ☐ 2×3^2

18. 25×10 ☐ $5^2 \times 5$

19. $10^3 - 560$ ☐ $10^2 - 56$

20. $5^2 \times 3$ ☐ 15×5

Go Further

21. Write three *Which is Greater* or *Write the Comparison* puzzles for a friend to solve.

_____

_____

_____

Friend's name _____

On today's activity: (Circle one) I need to know more. I got it.

Date

Today's Challenge — Ones-Digit Cycles

A *power* of a number is that number used as a factor a given number of times. The third power of two (2^3) is $2 \times 2 \times 2$. *Consecutive powers* of a number have exponents in counting order.

1. Fill in the table of consecutive powers of two. The first is done for you.

Exponential Form	Product
2^1	2
2^2	
2^3	
2^4	
2^5	
2^6	
2^7	
2^8	
2^9	

2. Fill in the table of consecutive powers of four.

Exponential Form	Product
4^1	
4^2	
4^3	
4^4	
4^5	
4^6	
4^7	
4^8	
4^9	

3. Fill in the table of consecutive powers of five.

Exponential Form	Product
5^1	
5^2	
5^3	
5^4	
5^5	
5^6	
5^7	
5^8	
5^9	

4. Fill in the table of consecutive powers of six.

Exponential Form	Product
6^1	
6^2	
6^3	
6^4	
6^5	
6^6	
6^7	
6^8	
6^9	

On today's activity: (Circle one) — I need to know more. — I got it.

Name   Date   157

Go Further — Ones-Digit Cycles

Work with a partner. Study the tables you filled in on page 157 and write any patterns or other interesting facts here or on another piece of paper.

Things we discovered: _____

_____

1. Fill in the table. The first is done for you.

2. Explain how you would find the ones digit for 6^{25}.

   _____

   _____

Consecutive Powers of	Ones-Digit Cycle
2	2, 4, 8, 6
4	
5	
6	

_____

3. Explain how you would find the ones digit for 2^{50}.

   _____

   _____

   _____

4. Do you think the ones-digit cycle for consecutive powers of four also works for consecutive powers of 14? Explain your reasoning and show a few examples.

   _____

   _____

   _____

5. What is special about the ones digits of powers of five and six? Explain.

   _____

   _____

   _____

On today's activity: (Circle one) — I need to know more. — I got it.

Get Started ✏ **Match the estimate with the strategy used to make it.**

_____ 1. 6279 + 752 → 6000 + 700 → 6700   **A.** Rounding both addends

_____ 2. 6279 + 752 → 6000 + 752 → 6752   **B.** Front-end

_____ 3. 6279 + 752 → 6300 + 800 → 7100   **C.** Compatible numbers

_____ 4. 6279 + 752 → 6275 + 750 → 7025   **D.** Rounding one addend

Go Further ✏ **Solve the riddles.**

5. **Clues:** • I am an estimate for 3932 + 512.

   • I was found by using a rounding strategy.

   • I am a number greater than 3000 and less than 4500.

   What number am I? _____

6. **Clues:** • I am an estimate for 6426 + 345.

   • I was found by using a compatible numbers strategy.

   • I am a number greater than 6700 and less than 6800.

   • What number am I? _____

7. Fill in the blanks to make and solve your riddle.

   Clues: • I am an estimate for _____ + _____ = _____.

   • I was found by using _____ strategy.

   • I am a number greater than _____ and less than _____.

   What number am I? _____

8. Now write your own riddle for a friend to solve.

   Clues: _____

   _____

   _____

   What number am I? _____

   Friend's name _____

On today's activity: (Circle one) ✏ I need to know more. ▪ I got it.

Name   **Date**   **159**

Get Started Circle the letters by the grids that will earn a point when they are machine scored. Explain why each choice will or will not work.

$1\frac{1}{2} \times 1\frac{2}{3} =$ _____ $2\frac{1}{2}$

A.  **B.**  **C.** 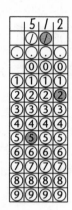 **D.**

A. _____

B. _____

C. _____

D. _____

Today's Challenge Fill in the grid with the correct product.

1. $3\frac{1}{2} \times 2$ **2.** $4\frac{1}{2} \times \frac{2}{5}$ **3.** $\frac{1}{2} \times \frac{3}{4}$ **4.** $18 \times \frac{3}{4}$

5. What advice would you give to a student trying to write fractions or mixed numbers into a test grid?

_____

_____

On today's activity: (Circle one) I need to know more. I got it.

160 Name

Date

Today's Challenge

Solve each problem. Then fill in the spaces below with the letter corresponding to each answer you found in order to spell out a message.

1.	K =	$3 \times 5^2 =$ _____	8.	A =	$3^3 \div 3^2 =$ _____
2.	O =	$3^2 - 2^3 =$ _____	9.	R =	$5^2 - 5 \times 2 =$ _____
3.	T =	$3^2 + 9^2 + 3^2 =$ _____	10.	H =	$3 \times 4 \times 5 =$ _____
4.	I =	$2^2 \times 2^2 + 8^2 =$ _____	11.	S =	$4^2 \div 8 =$ _____
5.	F =	$3^2 - 2^2 =$ _____	12.	D =	$100 - 7 \times 10 =$ _____
6.	C =	$9^2 - 9 =$ _____	13.	E =	$2 \times 5^2 + 5 =$ _____
7.	N =	$10^2 \div 10 =$ _____	14.	P =	$6 + 6^2 =$ _____

__ __ __ __ __   __ __ __ __ __   __ __
72 60 55 72 75   1 15 30 55 15   1 5

__ __ __ __ __ __ __ __ __ __
1 42 55 15 3 99 80 1 10 2

Go Further

15. Complete the table by raising each number to the second power.

x	1	2	3	4	5	6	7	8	9
x^2									

16. Describe any patterns you observe in the table.

_____

_____

_____

On today's activity: (Circle one) I need to know more. I got it.

Name   Date   **161**

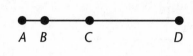

Today's Challenge ✏ Multiple Segments

1. Make a list of all the segments that are in this diagram. Explain how you are sure you have all possible segments in your list.

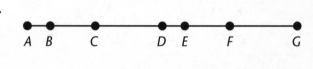

_____

_____

_____

2. List all of the segments in this diagram. Explain how you are sure you have all possible segments in your list.

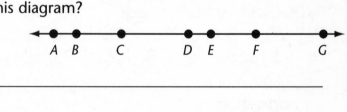

_____

_____

_____

3. How many rays can you name in this diagram? Explain how you are sure you have all possible rays in your list.

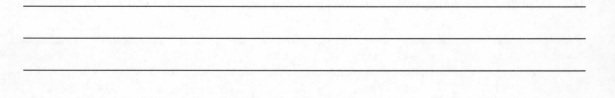

_____

_____

_____

_____

4. Explain why your answers to exercises 2 and 3 are not the same.

_____

_____

_____

On today's activity: (Circle one) ✏ I need to know more. ✏ I got it.

Date

Go Further — Multiple Segments

Suppose the problem from last time was a bit different. Instead of segments you are trying to figure out how many arcs can be drawn using points around the circumference of a circle. To name an arc smaller than a semicircle, use two letters.

1. How many different arcs do you see in this circle? Do *not* count the entire circle as an arc. What would you have to do to name these arcs?

_____

_____

2. How many different arcs arcs are in this circle?

_____

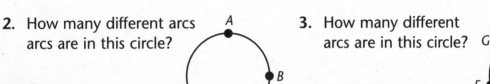

3. How many different arcs are in this circle?

_____

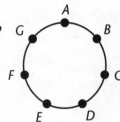

Things we discovered:

Work with a partner. Study your work on pages 162 and 163 to answer these questions.

4. Explain the differences among the number of segments formed by a given number of points on a segment, the number of rays formed by the same number of points on a line, and the number of arcs formed by the same number of points on a circle.

_____

_____

_____

5. What is a good way to organize the search for segments or arcs?

_____

_____

_____

On today's activity: (Circle one) — I need to know more. — I got it.

Name **Date** 163

Today's Challenge 🖎 Fill in the table.

1. $5 + {}^-8 =$ _____

2. ${}^-8 + 3 =$ _____

3. ${}^-11 + 3 =$ _____

4. $5 + {}^-12 =$ _____

5. $4 + {}^-9 =$ _____

6. $4 + {}^-2 =$ _____

7. ${}^-3 + {}^-1 =$ _____

8. $5 + {}^-5 =$ _____

9. $2 + 6 =$ _____

10. ${}^-6 + 3 =$ _____

11. ${}^-2 + 8 =$ _____

12. $6 + {}^-2 =$ _____

13. ${}^-6 + 8 =$ _____

14. $10 + {}^-4 =$ _____

15. ${}^-5 + 9 =$ _____

16. ${}^-7 + 3 =$ _____

17. ${}^-2 + {}^-5 =$ _____

18. ${}^-2 + 10 =$ _____

19. ${}^-8 + 8 =$ _____

20. ${}^-2 + {}^-6 =$ _____

On today's activity: (Circle one) 🖎 I need to know more. 🖎 I got it.

164 Name

Date

Get Started Fill in the letter of the correct answer. Here are four examples of Sue's work on a multiplication test. Mark the letter of each example that Sue has solved correctly, then correct her mistakes.

(A)   625
      × 403
    26,875

(B)   853
      × 213
   181,689

(C)   325
      × 614
   199,550

(D)   458
      × 203
    10,534

Today's Challenge Fill in the letter of the correct answer.

1. Mark the letter by the exercises do you think Sue would solve correctly. Find the correct products.

(A)   476
      × 356
    _____

(B)   732
      × 909
    _____

(C)   324
      × 325
    _____

(D)   833
      × 604
    _____

Find the products.

2. 635 × 405
   (A) 28,575
   (B) 257,175
   (C) 250,000
   (D) 28,000

3. 232 × 708
   (A) 164,256
   (B) 18,096
   (C) 164,260
   (D) 18,100

4. 623 × 904
   (A) 563,200
   (B) 563,192
   (C) 58,526
   (D) 58,562

5. 495 × 101
   (A) 5454
   (B) 5445
   (C) 49,995
   (D) 49,991

6. 668 × 803
   (A) 55,444
   (B) 536,606
   (C) 54,555
   (D) 536,404

7. 911 × 603
   (A) 549,333
   (B) 549,111
   (C) 57,393
   (D) 57,939

8. 458 × 302
   (A) 14,656
   (B) 14,565
   (C) 138,320
   (D) 138,316

9. 123 × 602
   (A) 74,046
   (B) 74,064
   (C) 7662
   (D) 7626

10. For which of exercises 2–9 could you choose the best answer without computing the exact product? _____

11. What advice would you give Sue about multiplying whole numbers?

_____

_____

On today's activity: (Circle one) I need to know more. I got it.

Name _____   **Date** _____   165

Today's Challenge
Choose answers from this box. You will not use all of the numbers in the box.

300
47
$\frac{7}{8}$
110
$\frac{2}{6}$
93
92
$\frac{3}{8}$
84
0.25
24
$\frac{15}{16}$
36
55

1. Find a fraction whose numerator is the only even prime number. _____

2. Find a square number between 26 and 48. _____

3. Find the greatest prime number that is less than 50. _____

4. Find a decimal that is equivalent to half of a half. _____

5. Find a number that is the product of the third prime number and the least two-digit prime number. _____

6. Find three more than half the number of degrees in the interior angles of a triangle. _____

7. Find a three-digit multiple of 100. _____

8. Find a two-digit number between 15 and 35 that is divisible by 2, 3, and 4. _____

9. Find the sum of $\frac{1}{2} + \frac{1}{4} + \frac{1}{8} + \frac{1}{16}$. _____

10. Find a fraction that is the mean of 0.25 and 0.5. _____

Go Further

11. Write the answers to exercises 1–10 in order from least to greatest.

_____

12. Find the difference between the greatest and least numbers in the box. _____

13. Find three numbers in the box whose sum is 226. _____

14. Use any numbers in the box and any operations. Write two different expressions whose value is 30.

_____

_____

On today's activity: (Circle one) I need to know more. I got it.

Date

Today's Challenge ▱ Searching for Triangles

This figure contains many triangles. Some are easier to see than others.

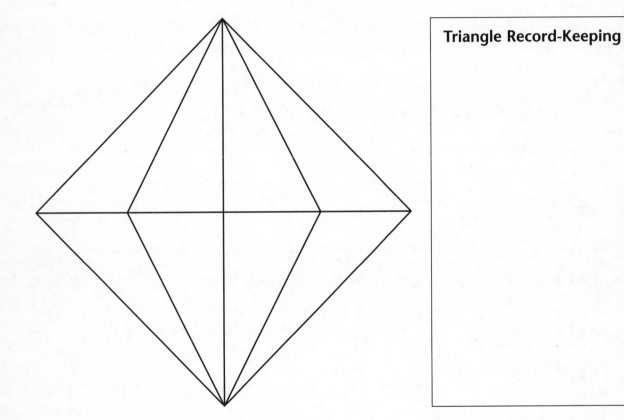

Triangle Record-Keeping

1. Make a search for all of the triangles in the figure. Before you start, decide how you will keep track of the triangles you find and how you will record them.

2. How many triangles are in the figure? _____

3. Explain how you know that you did not miss any triangles.

_____

_____

_____

On today's activity: (Circle one) ▱ I need to know more. ▱ I got it.

Name _____ **Date** _____ **167**

Go Further ✏ Searching for Triangles

Work with a partner. Study your work on page 167. Write any interesting patterns or other facts here or on another piece of paper.

Things we discovered: _____

_____

1. What is a good way to name triangles in a diagram?

   _____

2. What is a good strategy for organizing a search for overlapping figures?

   _____

   _____

3. Find all of the triangles in this figure. How many are there? _____

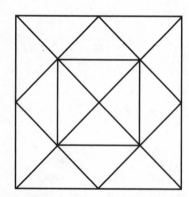

Triangle Record-Keeping

4. Explain how you know that you have counted all of the triangles.

   _____

   _____

5. How does your search strategy compare to the one you used on page 167?

   _____

   _____

On today's activity: (Circle one) ✏ I need to know more. ✏ I got it.

Date

Today's Challenge Use a string of four digits in one row or one column to write an expression using three different operations. Use the order of operations to find the value of the expression.

5	8	2	7
9	3	6	4
8	4	2	1
6	6	0	4

Expression _____

Value _____

_____ _____

_____ _____

_____ _____

_____ _____

Go Further Create your own Math Jumble. Have a friend use any row or any column in your Math Jumble to write an expression with three different operations. Have your friend write the expression and then find the value of the expression. If you disagree on expressions or values, check your work. Edit if necessary.

Expression _____

Value _____

_____ _____

_____ _____

_____ _____

_____ _____

Friend's name _____

On today's activity: (Circle one) I need to know more. I got it.

Name _____ **Date** _____ **169**

Get Started ✏ **Complete the analogy.** Choose the correct answer from the box. Draw it in the space provided.

[ ] is to ◿ as ◯ is to _____   [⊘ ⊘ ⊘ ⊘]

Explain why your choice is best and the other choices are incorrect.

_____

_____

Today's Challenge ✏ **Complete the analogy.** Choose the correct answer from the box. Write or draw it in the space provided.

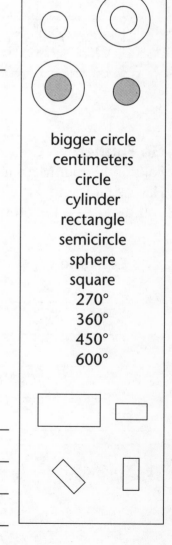

1. Perimeter is to triangle as circumference is to _____

2. [ ] is to [▓] as ◯ is to
   _____

3. Square is to cube as circle is to _____

4. △ is to ▷ as ▯ is to
   _____

5. Triangle is to 180° as quadrilateral is to _____

6. What advice would you give to a student taking his or her first analogies test?

_____

_____

_____

_____

bigger circle
centimeters
circle
cylinder
rectangle
semicircle
sphere
square
270°
360°
450°
600°

On today's activity: (Circle one) ✏ I need to know more. ✏ I got it.

170 **Name** _____

Date _____

Today's Challenge Find the next number in the sequence.

1. 6, 9, 12, 15, _____

2. 1, 3, 7, 15, _____

3. $\frac{1}{2}, \frac{2}{3}, \frac{3}{4}, \frac{4}{5},$ _____

4. 22, 19, 16, 13, _____

5. 1, 4, 9, 16, _____

6. 3, 4, 6, 9, _____

7. 5, 9, 13, 17, _____

8. 1, 3, 6, 10, _____

Go Further

9. Write five sequence problems, giving the first four numbers in the sequence.
Then ask a friend to find the next number in the sequence.

_____

_____

_____

_____

_____

10. Did your friend's answers match yours? If not, edit your problems
so there can be no confusion.

_____

_____

_____

_____

_____

Friend's name _____

On today's activity: (Circle one)   I need to know more.   I got it.

Name   **Date**

Today's Challenge — Four-Digit Product Challenge

Use the 2–9 digit cards to form four-digit factors. You are looking for the greatest possible product. Keep trying new combinations until you think you have found the greatest possible product. Remember, you can use each digit only once. Record your work here.

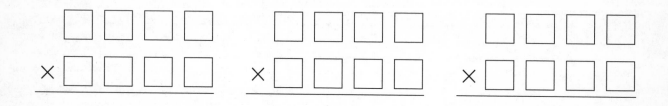

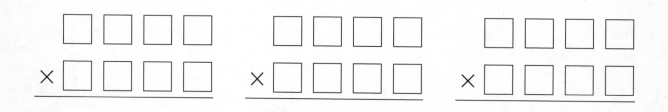

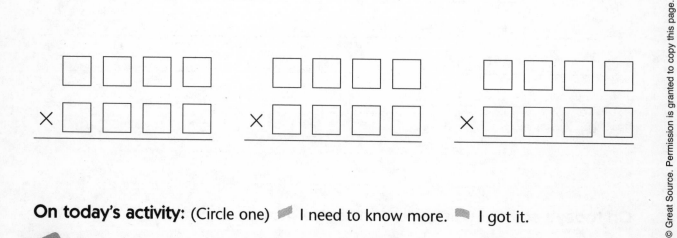

On today's activity: (Circle one) — I need to know more. — I got it.

172   **Name**

Date

Go Further — Four-Digit Product Challenge

You have probably found the greatest possible product for this challenge. Work with a partner to figure out what is true about your solution that is not true about other pairs of four-digit factors and their products.

Things we discovered: _____

_____

_____

_____

_____

_____

_____

_____

You can use what you learned from one problem to solve a related problem.

1. Describe why you believe your product is the greatest possible.

   _____

   _____

2. Arrange the digits 0–9 into two *five*-digit numbers with the greatest possible product. Record your work and explain your reasoning.

   _____

   _____

3. Arrange the digits 2–9 into two four-digit numbers with the *least* possible product. Record your work and explain your reasoning.

   _____

   _____

On today's activity: (Circle one) — I need to know more. — I got it.

Name   **Date**   173

Go Further   Follow the directions to mark numbers in the grid. Some numbers will be marked more than once.

35	6	21	48
94	72	18	42
78	45	60	86
24	16	32	70

1. Cross out all numbers greater than the number of minutes in an $1\frac{1}{4}$ hours.

2. Star all numbers that are multiples of the number of quarts in a gallon.

3. Circle all numbers that are less than the number of inches in $\frac{3}{4}$ of a yard.

4. Box all numbers that are divisible by the number of ounces in $\frac{3}{8}$ of a pound.

5. Underline all numbers that are multiples of the number of days in a week.

6. Which number is not marked? _____

7. Write at least three statements to describe that number.

_____

_____

_____

On today's activity: (Circle one)   I need to know more.   I got it.

Get Started Fill in the letter of the correct answer.

Expense	Percent of Budget
Housing	40%
Food	30%
Clothing	10%
Miscellaneous	20%

Which graph shows the results in the table?

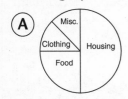 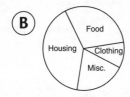 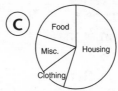 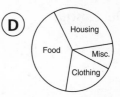

Today's Challenge Fill in the letter of the correct answer.

1. Which graph shows the results in the table?

Customer Type	Percent of Customers
Children under 12	50%
Adults	30%
Seniors	20%

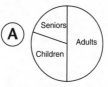 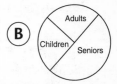

 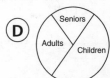

2. Which table best describes this graph?

A
Tree	Percent of Forest
White Oak	25%
Spruce	10%
Beech	30%
White Pine	5%
Maple	30%

B
Tree	Percent of Forest
White Oak	30%
Spruce	5%
Beech	10%
White Pine	25%
Maple	25%

C
Tree	Percent of Forest
White Oak	25%
Spruce	10%
Beech	5%
White Pine	30%
Maple	30%

D
Tree	Percent of Forest
White Oak	35%
Spruce	20%
Beech	5%
White Pine	35%
Maple	10%

3. For exercise 2, how did you decide which answer was best?

_____

4. What advice would you give to a student trying to read circle graphs showing percent?

_____

_____

_____

On today's activity: (Circle one) I need to know more. I got it.

Name **Date** 175

Today's Challenge
Fill in the rest of the table. Remember, perimeter of a circle is called *circumference*.

Figure	Dimensions	Area	Perimeter
Rectangle	length: 7 centimeters width: 5 centimeters	**1.**	**2.**
Square	**3.** side:	49 square centimeters	**4.**
Rectangle	**5.** length: width:	80 square centimeters	36 centimeters
Square	**6.** side:	**7.**	36 centimeters
Circle	radius: 10 centimeters	**8.**	**9.**
Circle	**10.** radius:	36π square centimeters	**11.**

Go Further

12. Draw and label diagrams of three different triangles with an area of 20 square centimeters. Use whole-number units.

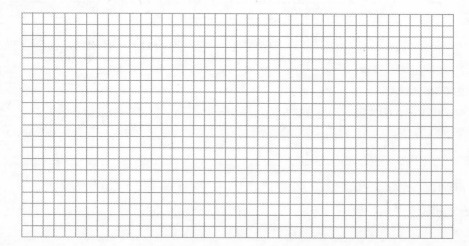

13. Relate your answer to exercise 12 to the factors for 40.

On today's activity: (Circle one) ⌐ I need to know more. ⌐ I got it.

Date

Today's Challenge — Ones-Digit Cycles

You can use what you learned about the ones-digit cycles of consecutive powers to solve these problems. Look back at pages 157–158 or use simpler numbers to help you establish the cycle of ones digits in consecutive powers of four, five, and six.

1. What is the ones digit of 4^{20}? _____   2. What is the ones digit of 5^{50}? _____

3. What is the ones digit of 6^{67}? _____

4. Use simpler numbers to discover the ones-digit cycles of consecutive powers, then find the ones digit for the indicated power. The first is started for you.

Consecutive Powers of	Use Simpler Numbers	Find the Ones Digit of
3	$3^1 = 3$	3^{45} _____
	$3^2 = 9$	
	3^3	
7		7^{30} _____
8		8^{75} _____
9		9^{100} _____

On today's activity: (Circle one) — I need to know more. — I got it.

Name   Date

Go Further — Ones-Digit Cycles

Work with a partner. Study your work for pages 157–158 and 177. Write any patterns and interesting facts you see.

Things we discovered: _____

_____

_____

_____

_____

You have learned that the ones digits of the consecutive powers of one-digit numbers form a cycle. Now you'll look at two-digit numbers.

1. Test consecutive powers of 75. Does the ones-digit cycle match the cycle for consecutive powers of five?

_____

_____

2. Test consecutive powers of 27. Does the ones-digit cycle match the cycle for consecutive powers of seven?

_____

_____

3. What is the ones digit for 38^{50}? Explain how you found it.

_____

_____

4. What is the ones digit of 365^{37}? Explain how you found it.

_____

_____

On today's activity: (Circle one) — I need to know more. — I got it.

178 Name _____

Date _____

Get Started ☞ **For each question, write *yes* or *no*.**

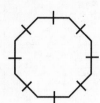

1. Is the figure a triangle? _____

2. Does it have any acute angles? _____

3. Does it have any right angles? _____

4. Do any of the angles measure more than 90 degrees? _____

5. Is the figure a quadrilateral? _____

6. Does it have any acute angles? _____

7. Does it have a line of symmetry? _____

8. Does it have any right angles? _____

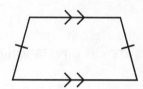

Go Further

9. Find more than one solution to this riddle.

   Clues: • I am a quadrilateral with an even number of sides.

   • I have at least one right angle.

   • I have at least one pair of parallel sides.

   What could be my name? _____

10. How would you change the clues for exercise 9 to make sure that it has only one possible solution?

    _____

    _____

11. Write your own riddle for a friend to solve.

    Clues: _____

    _____

    _____

    What is my name? _____

    Friend's name _____

On today's activity: (Circle one) ☞ I need to know more. ☞ I got it.

Name _____ **Date** _____

Get Started 🖋 **Complete the constructed response.**

Problem: Find the volume of a swimming pool 20 feet wide with this side view.

Solution:

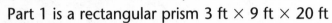

First, break up the problem into easy parts.
Show the parts on a diagram.

Next, find the volume of each part.

Part 1 is a rectangular prism 3 ft × 9 ft × 20 ft	$V = \ell wh$
	$= 3 \times 9 \times 20$
	$=$ **A.** _____
Part 2 is a rectangular prism 3 ft × 4 ft × 20 ft	$V = \ell wh$
	$=$ **B.** _____
	$= 240$
Part 3 is a rectangular prism 7 ft × 10 ft × 20 ft	$V = \ell wh$
	$= 7 \times 10 \times 20$
	$= 1400$
Part 4 is half of a rectangular prism 4 ft × 4 ft × 20 ft	$V =$ **C.** _____
	$= \frac{1}{2}(4 \times 4 \times 20)$
	$= \frac{1}{2}(320)$
	$= 160$

Find the sum of **D.** _____ . $540 + 240 + 1400 + 160 = 2340$

Last, carefully answer the original question.   The volume of this swimming pool is

E. _____ .

Today's Challenge 🖋 **Write a constructed response on a separate sheet of grid paper.**

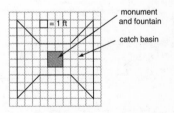

1. **Problem:** Find the volume of the catch basin of a fountain six feet deep with this top view.

2. What advice would you give to a student who wants to find the volume of an irregular figure?

_____

_____

_____

On today's activity: (Circle one) 🖋 I need to know more. 🖋 I got it.

Date

Match. Write the correct letter in the blank.

_____ **1.** the prime factorization of 54

_____ **2.** the greatest two-digit prime number

_____ **3.** the greatest common factor of 16 and 24

_____ **4.** the least common multiple of 10 and 12

_____ **5.** the least prime number

_____ **6.** a number divisible by four and five but not by three

_____ **7.** the prime factorization of 24

_____ **8.** the least common multiple of eight and 32

_____ **9.** the greatest two-digit multiple of three

_____ **10.** the whole number that is neither composite nor prime

a. 1.

b. 40

c. 99

d. 97

e. $2 \times 2 \times 2 \times 3$

f. 8

g. 60

h. 32

i. 2

j. 2×3^3

Fill in the blank for each question. Write fractions in simplest form.

11. Round 0.758 to the nearest tenth. _____

12. Round 1.4173 to the nearest thousandth. _____

13. Give a fraction equivalent to 75%. _____

14. Give the percent equivalent to $\frac{1}{20}$. _____

15. Give the decimal equivalent to $\frac{3}{8}$. _____

16. Name the first four prime numbers. _____

17. Write these numbers in order, least to greatest.

0.85, 5%, $\frac{1}{2}$, 62%, 0.1, 1.5, 100% _____

18. Write these numbers in order, least to greatest.

$^-10$, 0, $\frac{1}{4}$, $^-4$, $\frac{1}{2}$, $^-1$, $^-3$ _____

Name

Date

Fill in the circle for the best answer.

19. Which number is a fraction whose decimal equivalent repeats?

    (A) $\frac{1}{8}$ (B) $\frac{1}{7}$

    (C) $\frac{1}{4}$ (D) $\frac{1}{5}$

20. Which number is less than $\frac{1}{3}$ but greater than $\frac{1}{5}$?

    (A) $\frac{1}{6}$ (B) 50%

    (C) $\frac{1}{10}$ (D) 0.25

21. Which expression has the greatest value?

    (A) $2^2 \times 3^2$ (B) $2^3 \times 3$

    (C) $3^2 \times 2$ (D) 3^3

22. Which number is NOT equivalent to $33\frac{1}{3}$%?

    (A) $\frac{3}{9}$ (B) $0.\overline{3}$

    (C) 0.33   (D) $\frac{1}{3}$

23. The best estimate of 97×52.1 is

    (A) 5000   (B) 500

    (C) 450   (D) 4500

24. Label the sectors of this circle graph to match the information in the table.

Expense	Percent of Budget
Food	25%
Housing	40%
Clothing	20%
Miscellaneous	15%

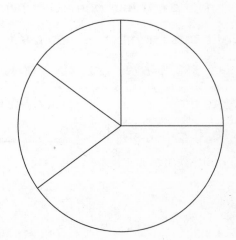

Fill in the circle of the best answer.

1. Which is the greatest?

   (A) $\frac{2}{3}$ of 390   (B) $\frac{3}{7}$ of 630

   (C) $\frac{4}{5}$ of 250   (D) $\frac{7}{10}$ of 400

2. Which is the least?

   (A) 25% of 200   (B) 10% of 550

   (C) $33\frac{1}{3}$% of 120   (D) 20% of 250

3. 75% of 60 is equivalent to

   (A) 4500×0.1 (B) $\frac{5}{9} \times 81$

   (C) $1.2 + 3.3$ (D) $46 - 1.5$

4. Which of the following is NOT equal to $\frac{5}{6} + \frac{1}{2}$?

   (A) $\frac{6}{8}$ (B) $\frac{4}{3}$

   (C) $\frac{8}{6}$ (D) $1\frac{1}{3}$

5. What is the product of 47.21 and 5.1?

   (A) 24.0771   (B) 240.771

   (C) 244.717   (D) 24.0717

6. The regular price of a sweater is $26 but it is on sale at 20% off. What is the sale price of the sweater?

   (A) $5.20   (B) $31.20

   (C) $20.80   (D) $23.40

7. $6(3 + 5)$ does NOT equal which of the following?

   (A) 48   (B) $18 + 30$

   (C) $6 \times 3 + 6 \times 5$ (D) $18 + 5$

8. Which expression has a value of 15?

   (A) $5 + 2 \times 8 - 3$ (B) $(5 + 2) \times 8 - 3$

   (C) $5 + (2 \times 8) - 3$ (D) $5 + 2 \times (8 - 3)$

Name   Date   183

Fill in the blank. Write fractions in simplest form.

9. 4501×0.01 _____

10. $1\frac{1}{2} + \frac{2}{3}$ _____

11. $5\frac{1}{2} \times \frac{2}{3}$ _____

12. $5 + ? = {}^{-}9$ _____

13. $5 \times 6 + 8 \div 2$ _____

14. ${}^{-}5 + 6$ _____

15. $12 + 2 \times 4 \times 3$ _____

16. Five is what percent of 20? _____

17. You buy an item for $2.35 and pay for it with a $5 bill. How much change will you receive? _____

18. You have saved $11.45. A video costs $19.95. How much more money do you need? _____

19. What is 10,000 less than 314,050? _____

20. What is 10^2 more than 999? _____

21. Pick a multiple of three between 20 and 29. _____

   Then add eight to that number. _____

   Divide that sum by the fraction $\frac{1}{2}$. _____

   Add six to that quotient. _____

   Subtract 22 from that sum. _____

   Divide that difference by two. _____

22. Complete the magic square using each of the digits 1–9 once. (Hint: Sums in rows, columns, and diagonals must be equal.)

		4
	5	
6		8

23.

$1\frac{9}{12}$	$\frac{1}{2}$	$1\frac{6}{8}$
$\frac{6}{12}$	$1\frac{3}{4}$	$\frac{7}{4}$
$\frac{2}{3}$	$\frac{1}{12}$	$\frac{3}{6}$

A. Cross out all the numbers equivalent to $\frac{5}{6} - \frac{1}{3}$.

B. Cross out all the numbers equivalent to $1\frac{1}{4} + \frac{1}{2}$.

C. Cross out all the numbers equivalent to $\frac{3}{8} \times \frac{2}{9}$.

   The only number NOT crossed out is _____.

trapezoid	square	equilateral triangle
kite		rhombus
parallelogram	quadrilateral	rectangle

For exercises 1–8, select from the box the best name for the polygon with the given attributes.

1. It has four congruent sides and no right angles. _____

2. It has two pairs of congruent adjacent
   sides and no parallel sides.   _____

3. All of the sides are congruent, and the sum
   of the measures of the angles is 180 degrees. _____

4. All of the sides are congruent, and it has a right angle. _____

5. Opposite sides are parallel, adjacent sides are not
   congruent, and there are no right angles.   _____

6. It has exactly one pair of parallel sides. _____

7. The sum of the angles is 360 degrees. _____

8. Opposite sides are parallel, there is a right angle,
   and there are exactly two lines of symmetry. _____

9. Write these polygon-names in order of the number of sides, least to greatest:
   hexagon, decagon, triangle, octagon, pentagon, quadrilateral, heptagon

   _____

10. How many diagonals does a pentagon have? _____

11. How many lines of symmetry does a square have? _____

Use this diagram for exercises 12 and 13. $\overset{A\quad B\quad\quad C}{\longleftrightarrow}$

12. Name all of the line segments defined in the diagram. _____

13. Name all of the rays defined in the diagram.

    _____

14. Name all of the arcs defined in the circle. Be sure
    to include major arcs other than the entire circle.

    _____

Name _____ **Date** _____ **185**

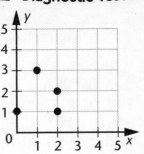

15. Choose the point that is NOT described by any of the following statements and state its coordinates. Label the other points with the appropriate capital letter.

A. $x = y$ **B.** It lies on the y axis.   **C.** $x > y$

16. How many triangles are defined in this diagram? _____

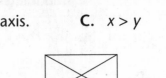

For exercises 17–20, complete the analogies.

17. A circle is to a sphere as a square is to a _____.

18. A picture frame is to a rectangle as a stop sign is to an _____.

19. A soup can is to a cylinder as a ball is to a _____.

20. A prism is to a pyramid as a _____ is to a cone.

21. Create a new magic square by rotating the one shown 90 degrees in a clockwise direction.

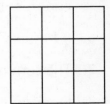

8	1	6
3	5	7
4	9	2

22. I am a polygon with the least possible even number of sides.
- I have one line of symmetry.
- I have one pair of parallel sides.
- I have congruent opposite non-parallel sides.

I am a (an) _____

23. Which two figures are reflections of each other?

(A)   (B)   (C)    (D)   (E)

24. Which figure will NOT fold into an open box?

(A)   (B)   (C)   (D)   (E)

25. Circle the triangle NOT described below and give its name. _____
Write the appropriate capital letter next to the others.

A. I am an acute isosceles triangle.

B. I am a right triangle.

C. I am an obtuse isosceles triangle.

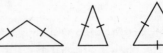

Match. Write the correct letter in the blank provided.

_____ 1. The number of minutes in $\frac{1}{10}$ of an hour.   **a.** 10

_____ 2. The number of gallons equivalent to 4 quarts.   **b.** 18

_____ 3. The number of minutes in 90 seconds.   **c.** 6

_____ 4. The number of inches in $1\frac{1}{2}$ feet.   **d.** $1\frac{1}{2}$

_____ 5. The number of quarts in eight cups.   **e.** 2

_____ 6. The number of inches in $\frac{3}{4}$ yard.   **f.** 1

_____ 7. The number of ounces in $\frac{5}{8}$ pound.   **g.** 27

For exercises 8–10, use these values: 16, 12, 16, 11, 15.

8. Find the mean. _____

9. Find the median. _____

10. Find the mode. _____

For exercises 11–14, use this line plot.

Number of Hours Students Studied for Exam

11. How many students are represented in this line plot? _____

12. What is the mode? _____

13. What is the median? _____

14. What is the mean? _____

15. The area of a rectangle is 24 square inches and its width is three inches. Find the length. _____

16. The perimeter of a rectangle is 24 inches and its width is three inches. Find the length. _____

17. Laurie's plane leaves at 2:45 P.M. If it is 11:10 A.M. now, how many hours and minutes does Laurie have before the plane leaves?

_____

Name   **Date**

For exercises 18 and 19, use this triangle.

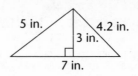

5 in.   4.2 in.   3 in.   7 in.

18. Find the number of inches in the perimeter of the triangle and fill in your answer on the appropriate grid.

19. Find the number of square inches in the area of the triangle and fill in your answer on the appropriate grid.

18.

19.

For exercises 20–25, fill in the circle of the correct answer. Use the diagram.

20. Find the perimeter of the parallelogram.

11 m
3.8 m
5 m

   (A) 15.4 meters   (B) 32 meters

   (C) 15.4 square meters   (D) 32 square meters

21. Find the area of the parallelogram.

   (A) 32 meters   (B) 55 square meters

   (C) 4l.8 square meters   (D) 20.9 meters

20 ft

22. Find the circumference of the circle.

   (A) 10π feet   (B) 20 feet

   (C) 100π square feet   (D) 20π feet

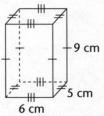

9 cm
5 cm
6 cm

23. Find the area of the circle.

   (A) 100π square feet   (B) 400π square feet

   (C) 20π square feet   (D) 10π square feet

24. Find the total surface area of the rectangular solid.

   (A) 258 centimeters   (B) 270 centimeters

   (C) 258 square centimeters   (D) 270 square centimeters

25. Find the volume of the rectangular solid.

   (A) 259 square centimeters   (B) 258 cubic centimeters

   (C) 270 square centimeters   (D) 270 cubic centimeters

Name

Date

Match each sequence with the next three terms in the sequence.

_____ 1. 2, 4, 8, 16

_____ 2. 12, 9, 6, 3

_____ 3. 7, 9, 12, 16

_____ 4. 1, 12, 23, 34

a. 0, ⁻3, ⁻6

b. 45, 56, 67

c. 32, 64, 128

d. 21, 27, 34

5. Choose the expression that is NOT equivalent to 21×19.

(A) $(20 \times 19) + (1 \times 19)$

(B) $(21 \times 20) - (21 \times 1)$

(C) $(10 \times 19) + (11 \times 19)$

(D) $(31 \times 19) + (10 \times 19)$

6. Which of the following expressions is NOT equivalent to 16?

(A) $2(x + 8)$, where $x = 1$

(B) $x^2 + 7$, where $x = 3$

(C) $8(x - 4)$, where $x = 6$

(D) $5x - 4$, where $x = 4$

For exercises 7 and 8, choose the greatest common factor. Use it and the Distributive Property to rewrite the expression.

7. $333x + 27$ _____

(A) 1
(B) 3
(C) 9
(D) 27

8. $30x - 25xy$ _____

(A) 5
(B) x
(C) $5x$
(D) $5xy$

For exercises 9–11, write an algebraic expression.

9. The sum of twice a number and seven. _____

10. The difference of twelve and a number. _____

11. The quotient in which the dividend is six
and the divisor is five times a number. _____

For exercises 12–15, solve the equation.

12. $x + 12 = 17$ _____

13. $6x = 24$ _____

14. $3x - 8 = 16$ _____

15. $7x + 8 = 36$ _____

For exercises 16 and 17, solve the proportion.

16. $\frac{3}{7} = \frac{n}{63}$ _____

17. $\frac{5}{6} = \frac{40}{n}$ _____

Name

Date

18. A recipe that calls for three cups of broth will feed eight people. If a club wishes to feed 40 people, how many cups of broth will be needed? _____

19. If a 1–6 number cube is rolled, what is the probability of a five landing face up? _____

20. If a 1–6 number cube is rolled, what is the probability that a five will NOT land face up? _____

For exercises 21–23, use the tree diagram.

21. Name all of the possible outcomes if two coins are tossed.

    _____

22. What is the probability that both coins will be heads? _____

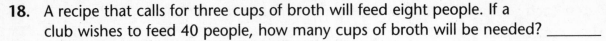

First Toss   Second Toss

23. A game is designed as follows: Two coins are tossed. You win if they match. Your partner wins if they do not match. Is this a fair game? Why or why not?

_____

For exercises 24–26, use this table to decide whether the statement was true or false when the table was published.

Imports from selected countries into the United States

Country	Imports (in billions of dollars)
Canada	217.0
Japan	126.6
Taiwan	33.4
United Kingdom	41.4

Source: U.S. Census bureau, Foreign Trade Division

T F 24. The imports from Taiwan were about three-fourths those of the United Kingdom.

T F 25. The United States had about three times as many imports from Japan as from Taiwan.

T F 26. More than half of the total imports represented here were from Canada.

27. New squares are formed, as shown, by dividing the side lengths by two. Some results are shown in the table. Complete the table.

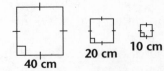

20 cm   10 cm

40 cm

Side (in centimeters)	Perimeter (in centimeters)	Area (in square centimeters)
40	160	1600
20	80	400
10	40	100
	20	
		6.25
n		

Date